# OLD TESTAMENT

# RULERS IN THE
# ERA OF MONARCHY

## LUCILLE ZAYAS

No part of this book may be reproduced, stored in a retrieval system or transmitted by any means, electronic, mechanical, photocopying, recording or otherwise, without written permission from the author.

ISBN: 0-9745188-7-5
Library of Congress Control Number: 2004112440

© 2004 by Lucille Zayas. All Rights Reserved.
This book is printed on acid free paper.
Printed in the United States of America

Publisher:     **Fishbowl International, Inc.**
               *"Viewing Life from all Angles"*
               PO Box 362
               Roxie, MS
               **www.fishbowlinternational.com**

# Previous works by Lucille Zayas

Knowing and Teaching the Old Testament, 2004

**Lovingly and gratefully dedicated**
To my four grandchildren:

Micah Coger
Jamar Coger
Reggie Zayas Jr.
NeAva P. Zayas

# RULERS IN THE
# ERA OF MONARCHY

**LUCILLE ZAYAS**

# Fishbowl
## International, Inc.

# FOREWORD

The *Era* of *Monarchy* will cover the four Kings Books of the Old Testament. I Samuel relates in detail the closing days of theocracy in which God ruled directly through the Judges and the early days of the Kingdom. The first two books I and II Samuel cover the first King, Saul, he was not a man after God's own heart. At his death after a long reign, David, God's own choice as king, was proclaimed ruler. These two books speak of the last days of the account of Samuel, the reign and the death of Saul and King David reign.

I and II Kings continue the history of the people of Israel from the accession of Solomon, David's son, to the carrying away of the people into captivity. I Kings record the death of David, the accession of Solomon, the revolt of Jeroboam and the ten-tribes and the narrative intermingle histories of the two kingdoms up to the captivity of each. The lives of the prophets Elijah and Elisha are also found in these books.

I and II Chronicles are, to a large extent, a repetition of matter found in other parts of the scriptures. The first nine chapters give a genealogy, or list of names beginning with Adam. The author lays most stress on the history of the kingdom of Judah, with special reference to the temple worship.

# Contents

# Introduction

Nearly four hundred years from the time of Exodus and over eight hundred years from the making of God's covenant with Abraham, the Israelites requested a human king to lead them, as other nations had monarchs. Their request constituted a rejection of God's own kingdom over them (I Samuel 8:4-8). The rule of God over Israel in a theocratic nation was ideal. God allowed Israel to have a king even when the people choice signified rejection of Him. Samuel prayed for direction in the confusing situation. (I Samuel 8:6-22). The Kingdom went from "United," "Divided" and then Single which was Judah-Southern Kingdom.

**An Approach to Study the Kings**
1. Statements about each king is followed by a biblical scripture; Reproof them with your Bible.
2. There are four kings book covering the twenty kings of Israel and the twenty kings of Judah, including the Queen Athaliah.
   (a) I Samuel – also known as the I Kings book (beginning 8:4-8)
   (b) II Samuel – also known as the II Kings book.
   (c) I Kings – also known as the III Kings book.
   (d) II Kings – also known as the IV kings book
   (e) I Chronicles and II Chronicles cover the lineage and the "affairs of the day."
3. The Empire's king that also played apart in the history of the kings:
   (1) Babylonian Empire
   (2) Assyrian Empire
   (3) Egyptian Rulers
   (4) Syrian Rulers

# Rulers in the Era of the Monarchy

- SAUL (32)
- *# DAVID (40)
- *SOLOMON (40)

UNITED
KINGDOM

---

| Southern Kings | Northern Kings |
|---|---|
| • **REHOBOAM (17)** | •#JEROBOAM I (22) |
| ABIJAM (3) | NADAB (2) |
| * ASA (41) | #BAASHA (24) |
| * JEHOSHAPHAT (25) | ELAH (2) |
| | # ZIMRI (7 days) |
| JEHORAM (8) | •# OMRI (11) |
| AHAZIAH (1) | TIBNI (3) |
| | • AHAB (22) |
| | AHAZIAH(2) |

DIVIDED
KINGDOM

| | |
|---|---|
| •ATHALIAH (7) | JEHORAM (12) |
| | •# JEHU (28) |
| * JOASH (40) | JEHOAHAZ (17 |
| | JEHOASH (16) |
| AMAZIAH (29) | JEROBOAM 11 (41) |
| *UZZIAH (52) | ZECHARIAH (6 mos.) |
| * JOTHAM (16) | # SHALLUM (1 mos.) |
| AHAZ (16) | # MENAHEM (10) |
| | PEKAHIAH (2) |
| * HEZEKIAH (29) | # PEKAH (20) |
| | # HOSHEA (10) |

2

**HEZEKIAH**
- **MANASSEH (55)**
  **AMON(2)**
* **JOSIAH (31)**                                    **SINGLE**
                                                     **KINGDOM**

  **JEHOAHAZ (3mos)**
  **JEHOIAKIM (11)**
  **JEHOIACHIN (3 mos.)**
- **ZEDEKIAH (11)**

( ) = YEARS OF THE KING'S REIGN
 * = GOOD KINGS  -  BASICALLY RIGHTEOUS
•= KINGS WHO PARTICULARLY INFLUENCED HISTORY
# = FOUNDERS OF A DYNASTY

# Period of The Kingdoms

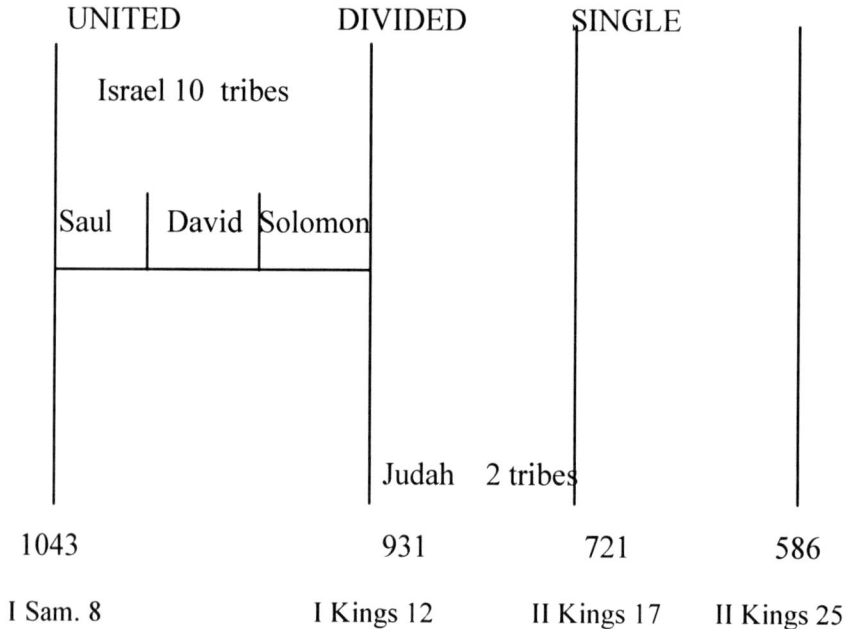

|  | UNITED | DIVIDED | SINGLE |  |
|---|---|---|---|---|

Israel 10 tribes

Saul | David | Solomon

Judah    2 tribes

| 1043 |  | 931 | 721 | 586 |
|---|---|---|---|---|
| I Sam. 8 |  | I Kings 12 | II Kings 17 | II Kings 25 |

# Period of the Kingdom

**Israelite Kings** (Northern Kingdom) (Ten – Tribes)

God initially ruled Israel as an invisible King through various agencies, first through Moses and then through human judges from Joshua to Samuel (Judges 8:23; I Samuel 12:12). Eventually the Israelites clamored for a king so as to be like the nations around them. (I Samuel 8:5-8, 19) under the legal provision embodied in the Law covenant for a divinely appointed human king, God appointed Saul of the tribe of Benjamin through the prophet Samuel. (Deuteronomy 17:14-20; I Samuel 9:15, 16; 10:21, 24) because of disobedience and presumptuousness Saul

4

lost God favor and the opportunity to provide a dynasty of Kings. (I Samuel 13:1-14, 15:22-28).

## Judean Kings (Southern Kingdom) (Two-Tribes)

Turning then to the tribe of Judah, God selected David the son of Jesse to be the next King of Israel. (I Samuel 16:13: 17:12). For faithfully supporting God's worship and Laws David was privileged to establish a dynasty of kings. (II Samuel 7:15, 16). The Israelites reached a peak of prosperity under the reign of Solomon, a son of David – 1 King 4:25; II Chronicle 1:15.

During the reign of Solomon, the nation was split into two kingdoms. The first king of the Northern, Ten-Tribe Kingdoms, generally spoken of as Israel was Jeroboam the son of Nebat of the tribe of Ephraim. (I Kings 11:26; 12:20) Disobediently he turned the worship of his people to golden calves. For this sin he came under God's disfavor (I Kings 14:10, 16). A total of twenty kings ruled in the Northern Kingdom from 997 to 740 BC, beginning with Jeroboam and ending with Hoshea the son of Pekah.
In the Southern Kingdom, Judah, nineteen kings reigned from 997 to 607 BC, beginning with Rehoboam and ending with Zedekiah (Athaliah a Usurper of the throne and not a king, is not counted.

The Judean Kingdom was conquered by the Babylonian in 586 BC (II Kings 25).

# A Comparison of the Two Kingdoms

|  | NORTH | SOUTH |
|---|---|---|
| **NAME:** | Israel | Judah |
| **FIRST KING:**<br>**TRIBES:**<br>**DURATION:** | Jeroboam<br>10<br>209 Years | Rehoboam<br>2<br>345 |
| **\*DYNASTIES:**<br>**KINGS**<br>**CAPITAL:** | 9<br>20<br>Samaria | 1<br>20<br>Jerusalem |
| **CONQUERED BY:**<br>**CONQUERED IN:**<br>**LAST KING:** | Assyria<br>721 B.C.<br>Hoshea | Babylon<br>605 B.C.<br>Zedekiah |

\*<u>Southern Kingdom</u>

(1) David (II Samuel; I Kings 1:1-2:10; I Chronicle 11:;29)

\*<u>Northern Kingdom</u>

(1) Jeroboam's Dynasty-Jeroboam fortified Shechem and made it the first capitol of the North (I King 12:25, I King 11:26-40; 12:15-14, 20; 15:25-28.
(2) Baasha (I Kings 15:27- 16:20).
(3) Zimri (I Kings 15:27-16:20).
(4) The Dynasty of Omri (I Kings 16:21-22:40; II Kings 1:1 – 9:26).

(5) The Dynasty of Jehu ( II Kings 9:1-10:26; 13:1-25, 14:8-16, 23, 24; 15:8-12).
(6) Shallum ( II Kings 15:8, 10-15)
(7) Menahem ( II Kings 15:22)
(8) Pekah (II Kings 15:32, 37, 38)
(9) Hoshea (II Kings 17:1, 2,3-6)

# UNITED KINGDOM

## 1. King Saul

## 2. King David

## 3. King Solomon

# King Saul

Reign 32 Years

The first divinely selected king of Israel ( I Samuel 9:15, 16;10:1) a Benjamite, son of Kish. Saul, an impressive young man without equal amount the Israelites – a head taller than any of the others.

The name of Saul's wife was Ahinoam. Saul fathered at least seven sons, Jonathan, Ishui, Malchi-Shua, Abinadad, Ishbosheth (Eshbaal), Armoni and Mephibosheth and two daughters, Merab and Michal. Abner evidently King Saul's uncle served as Chief of the Israelite army. (I Samuel 14:49, 50; II Samuel 2:8; 21:8: I Chronicle 8:33).

God having, in the law, undertaken to choose their King (Deuteronomy 17:15), they all sit still, till they heard from heaven. The chapter nine unfolds with a short account of Saul's parentage and person (I Samuel 9:1, 2). A large account of bringing Saul to Samuel. (Verses 3-6). Samuel being informed of God concerning him (Verse 7) treated him with respect (Verse 27).

Saul was anointed as king. To confirm that God was with Saul, Samuel gave him three prophetic signs, all of which were fulfilled that day. (I Samuel 9:22-10:16).
Saul lived during a turbulent time of Israel's history. Philistine oppression had reduced the nation to a helpless state militarily. (I Samuel 9:16), and the Ammonites under King Nahash threatened aggression (I Samuel 12:12).

Saul was rejected by God –Saul transgressed God's command by sparing the best of their flock and herd and King Agag. When asked why he had not obeyed God's voice, Saul disclaimed guilt and shifted the blame onto the people. There he has sin and was rejected by God as king.

Saul Slain – In the ensuring conflict with the Philistines, Saul was severely wounded at Mount Gilboa and three of his sons were slain. As his armor bearer refused to put him to death, Saul fell upon his own sword. (I Samuel 31:1-7). About three days later a young Amalekite came to David boasting that he had put the wounded king to death. This was evidently a lie, designed to gain David's favor, David, however, commanded that the man be executed for claiming to have killed God's anointed. (II Samuel 1:1-15).

Meanwhile the Philistine had fastened the corpses of Saul and his three sons on the wall of Beth Shan. Courageous men of Jabesh-Gilead, however, retrieved the bodies, buried them and then burned the bones. (I Samuel 31:8-13).

# KING DAVID

Reign 40 Years

David as King began after the tragic death of Saul. After being a fugitive from Saul, he saw Saul as God's anointed one and he loved Jonathan, Saul son.

David now moved to Hebron, at the age of thirty, the older men of Judah anointed him over the tribe in 1077 BC. Saul son Ishbosheth was made king of the other tribes. About two years later Ishbosheth was assassinated, his assailants bringing his head to David hoping to receive a reward, but they too were put to death like the pretended killer of Saul (II Samuel 2:1-4, 8-10; 4:5-12). This paved the way for the tribe who had until then supported Saul's son to join Judah and in time, a force, numbering 340,822 rallied made David king of all Israel (II Samuel 5:1-3: I Chronicle 11:1-3; 12:23-40). David ruled at Hebron seven and a half years before moving his capital, at God's direction, to the captured Jebusite stronghold, Jerusalem. There he built the city of David on Zion and continued to rule another thirty-three years (II Samuel 5:4-10; I Chronicle 11:4-9, II Chronicle 6:6). While living at Hebron, King David took more wives, after Michal returned, he fathered a number of sons and daughters (II Samuel 3:2-5, 13-16; I chronicle 3:1-4). After moving to Jerusalem, David acquired more wives and concubines who, in turn, bore him more children (II Samuel 5:13-16); I Chronicle 14:3-7). When the Philistines heard that David was king of all Israel, they came to overthrow him, as in the past. (I Samuel, 23:2-4, 10-12; 30:8) David inquired of God as to whether he should go against them. "Go Up," was the answer, and God burst upon the enemy with such overpowering destruction that David called the place Baal-Perazion, meaning "Master of Breaking Through." In a return encounter God's strategy shifted and David was ordered to circle around and strike the Philistines from the rear (I Chronicle 14:8-17; II Samuel 5:17-25). David attempted to bring the Ark of Covenant to Jerusalem, but this failed when Uzzah touched it and was struck down. (II Samuel 6:2-10; I Chronicle 13:1-14) some three months later, with careful preparations, including sanctifying the priest and Levites and making sure the Ark was carried on their shoulders instead of being placed in a wagon as at first, it was brought to Jerusalem. David simply clad, showing his joy and enthusiasm on this great occasion by "leaping and dancing around before God." But his wife Michal chided David, saying he acted "just as one of the empty-headed men" for this unjustified complaint Michal "came to have no children" down to the day of her death. (II Samuel 6:11-23; I Chronicle 15:1-29).

David also arranged for expanded worship of God at the Ark's new location by assigning gate keepers and musicians and seeing that there were "burnt offerings"…. Constantly "morning and evening" (I Chronicle 16:1-6; 37-43) in addition, David thought of building a temple-palace of cedar to house the Ark, to replace its tent. But David was not permitted to build the house, for God said: "Blood in great quantity you have spilled on the earth before me" (I Chronicle 22:8; 28:3). However, God make a covenant with him promising that the kingship would everlastingly remain in his family, an in connection with this covenant God assured him that his son Solomon whose name mean "peaceable," would build the temple. (II Samuel 7:1-16, 25-29; I Chronicle 17:1-27, II Chronicle 6:7-9, Psalms 89:3-4, 35-36) but God permitted David to expand his territory, maintaining peace with many Kings and conquering opponents. There God given victories made David a powerful ruler (I Chronicle 14:17).

**Sins bring calamity** After learning that Bathsheba husband was off to war, David entertained wrong desires by observing her from the rooftop, beautiful Bathsheba was bathing. David had her brought to his palace where he had relationship with her. The king was later notified that she was pregnant. When Bathsheba husband refused to spend the night with his wife, David has his captain to put Uriah on the front line where he would be killed. Many other sins reached it peak throughout David's family. (See II Samuel 12th Chapter through the 15th Chapter).

**End of David's reign** In the closing days of David's life the seventy-year old king now confined to his bed, continued to reap calamity within his family. (I Kings 1:5-48; I Chronicle 28:5;

29:20-25; II Chronicle 1:8). David then counseled Solomon to walk in God's way, keep his statues and commandments, act prudently in everything, and then he would prosper (I Kings 2:1-9). After a forty-year reign David died and was buried in the city of David, having proved worthy in faith (I Kings 2:10-11; I Chronicle 29:26-30; Hebrew 11:32).

Other Events in David's Life
- Private anointing of David, I Samuel 16:1-13
- David becomes Saul minstrel,I Samuel 16:14-23
- David and Goliath,I Samuel 17:4-58
- Davids marriage to Michal,I Samuel 18:20-30
- David's outlaw life from Saul (7 years),I Samuel 21:1-26
- David spares Saul's life (skirt, I Samuel 26:1-25
- David and Nabal-, I Samuel 25:1-44
- The spear and the cruse incident, I Samuel 26:1-25
- David among the Philistines,I Samuel 27:1-31:13
- David Mourn over the death of Saul and Jonathan
- David becomes King in Judah,II Samuel 2:1-7
- War between David and Ish-busheth, I Samuel 2:8-11
- David King over all Israel/, II Samuel 5:1-24
- Jerusalem becomes Capital, II Samuel 5:1-16
- Ark brought to Jerusalem, II Samuel 6:1-23
- Birth of Solomon, II Samuel 12:24, 25
- Preparation for building the temple, II Samuel 7:1-29
- Absalom's rebellion, II Samuel 13:1-9-5:12
- Solomon anointed and proclaimed
- Death of David

# King Solomon

Reign 40 Years

Solomon, Son of King David of the line of Judah. King of Israel from 1037 to 997 BC. The Bible record, after reporting the death of the son born to David through his illicit relations with Bathsheba, continues: "and David began to comfort Bathsheba his wife." He came in to her and lay down with her and she bore a son, and his name came to be called Solomon (peaceable) (II Samuel 12:24-25).

God had declared to David, before Solomon's birth, that a son would be born to him and that his name would be Solomon, and that this one would build a house in His name. The name Solomon (peaceable) applied in connection with the Covenant that God made with David, being a man who had shed much blood in warfare, would not build the house for God. (I Chronicle 22:6-10).

After Solomon's birth, his name appeared again at the time of David's old age. David, doubtless on account of God's promise, had previously sworn to Bathsheba that Solomon would succeed him on the throne. This was known to the prophet Nathan (I Kings 1:11-13, 17) whether Solomon's half brother Adonijah knew of his oath or intent of David, is not stated. In any case, Adonijah made an attempt to gain the throne in a manner similar that used by Absolom. Perhaps because of the King's feebleness and because Adonijah had the support of Joab the Army Chief and Abiathar the Priest, he had confidence that he would be successful. It was nonetheless a treasonable action, an effort to seize the throne while David was still alive and without the approval of David or of God (I Kings 1:5-10).

The prophet Nathan, ever faithful to God and to David, was on the alert about Adonijah. First sending Bathsheba with instructions to inform the king of the plot. David acted quickly calling for Zadok the Priest and Nathan to take Solomon to Gihon under the protection of Benaiah and his men. He was to put Solomon on the King's own she-mule (denoting a high honor to the one riding in this case, that he was successor to the kingship). David's instructions were followed out and Solomon was anointed, and acclaimed as king. (I Kings 1:11-40). On hearing the sound of the music at Gihon, not so very far away, and shouting of the people: "Let King Solomon live," Adonijah and his conspiracy fled in fear. Solomon did not execute revenge on Adonijah but instead Solomon sent to the Sanctuary where Adonijah had fled for asylum and had Adonijah brought before him. Informing Adonijah that if he shows himself to be a worthy man, he could live. (I Kings 1:41-53).

David, before dying, gave Solomon the Solemn charge to "keep the obligation to God by walking in His ways, by keeping His statutes, His commandments and His judicial decisions and His testimonies. He further instructed him concerning Joab and Shimei not to let them "go down into Sheol in peace": also to show loving kindness toward the sons of Barzillai the Gileadite. (I Kings 2:1-9) Solomon was again anointed as King and Zadok as Priest (I Chronicle 22:6-19).
Adonijah seditious request came up despite the mercy Solomon had shown him, and it was not long before Solomon had to act to carry out David's instruction concerning Joab and Shimei put to death (I Kings 2:13-25). Adonijah was put to death by Benaiah and later depose of the priest Abiathar and then Joab and Shimei put to death. (I King 2:26-46).

In the early part of Solomon's reign the people were sacrificing on many "high places," because there was no house of God although the tabernacle was at Gibeon and the Ark of the Covenant was in a tent on Zion. (I Kings 3:2-3). God appeared to Solomon in a dream, saying: "Request what I should give you." Instead of asking for riches, glory and victory, Solomon requested a wise, understanding and obedient heart in order to be able to judge Israel. Solomon humble request pleased God so that He gave him, not only what he had asked for but also riches and glory "so that there will not have happened to be any other among the Kings like you, all your days." And God also added the Admonition: "And if you will walk in my ways by keeping my regulations and my commandments, just as David your father walked, I will lengthen your days" (I Kings 3:4-14) . Solomon first judicial wisdom came when the two prostitutes presented a problem of paternity identity (I Kings 3:16-28).

In the fourth year of Solomon's reign, in the second month of the year in 1034 BC, Solomon began to build the house of God on Mount Moriah. (I Kings 6:1). The building of the temple was peacefully quiet: The stones were fitted before being brought to the site, so that no sound of hammers or axes of any tools were heard. ( I Kings 6:7). King Hiram, selected by David with architectural plan and Hiram cooperated in supplying timbers of cedar and Juniper trees in exchange for wheat and oil. (I Kings 5: II Chronicle 2:17-18). The tremendous building project occupied seven and a half years being concluded in the eight month in 1027 BC (I Kings 6:37-38). It appears that it took some time afterward to bring in the utensils and to get everything arranged, for it was in the seventh month, Ethanim, at the time of the festival of booths, that the sanctification and the inauguration of the temple were carried out by Solomon. (I Kings 8:2, II Chronicle 7:8-10). At the inauguration all the priest officiated: The service was carried out like David arranged (II Chronicle 5:11). Solomon later set the divisions of the priest over their services and the Levites in their posts of duty as it had been outlined by David. The temple now became the place where all Israel was to gather for their seasonal festivals and their sacrifices to God. Solomon during his thirteen year after completing the temple built a royal palace (a government building) and then a nationwide building (I Kings 9:20-22; II Chronicle 8:7-10). Solomon engaged extensively in trade for he had riches and glory for there was no king in all the earth possessing the riches of Solomon. (I Kings 10:23, II Chronicle 9:22). Solomon's throne exceeded in significance the way it was laid ( I Kings 10:18-20; II Chronicle 9:17-19) the same for his household food supply ( I Kings 4:1-22, 27, 28). Probably the most distinguished visitor that came from lands to view the riches and glory of Solomon was the Queen of Sheba. The Queen observed the splendor of the temple and Solomon's house, his table and drinking service and the attire of his waiters and the regular burnt offering at the temple. Then she bestowed upon Solomon the magnificent gift of 120 talents of gold (about $4,639,320.00) and a great number of precious stones, and balsam oil in unusually great quantity. Solomon in turn gave the

Queen whatever she asked. (I Kings 10:10, 13, II Chronicle 9:9, 12).

God continued to give Solomon wisdom, he uttered the books of Proverbs, Ecclesiastes, Song of Solomon (and at least one of Psalms, namely Psalm 127). Solomon was faithful to God until he started loving many foreign women and married the daughters of Pharoah, Moabite, Ammonite, Edomite, Sidonian and the Hittite women. He came to have seven hundred wives, princesses and three hundred concubines; and his wives gradually inclined his heart. And it came about in the time of Solomon's growing old that his wives themselves had inclined his heart to follow other gods. (I Kings 11:1-8).

The Length of Solomon reign was forty years (I Chronicle 29:1, II Chronicle 9:30). Because of Solomon's deviation from righteousness, God began to raise up resisters to Solomon, primarily Jeroboam of the tribe of Ephraim, who finally pulled ten tribes away from loyalty to the throne in Rehoboam's time and who established the Northern Kingdom that came to be called Israel. Other enemy of David gave trouble to Solomon (I Kings 11:14-40, 12-15) after Solomon death Rehoboam, Solomon's son ruled.

# Other Events of Solomon's Kingdom

- Solomon becomes real King, I Kings 2:1-46
- Wisdom given to Solomon, I Kings 3:1-28; 4:29-34
- Temple foundation laid, I Kings 6
- Temple dedicated, I Kings 7 Chapter and 8 Chapter
- Visit of Queen Sheba, I Kings 10:1-13
- The marriages of Solomon (foreign women) , I Kings 11:1-8
- The Kingdom split (Divided Kingdom) (Judah-two tribes, Israel ten tribes), I Kings 11
- Jeroboam flees to Shishak in Egypt, I Kings 11:40
- Death of Solomon, I Kings 11:41

# **Divided Kingdom**
## (Kings of Israel) Northern Kingdom (Ten Tribes)

1.    Jeroboam I

2.    Nadab

3.    Baasha

4.    Elah

5.    Zimri

6.    Omri

7.    Tibni

8.    Ahab

9.    Ahaziah

10.    Jehoram

11.    Jehu

12.    Jehoahaz

13.    Jehoash

14.    Jeroboam II

15.    Zechariah

16.    Shallum

17.    Menahem

18.    Pekahiah

19.    Pekah

20.    *Hoshea


*The last King before the fall of the Northern Kingdom

# King Jeroboam

Reign 22 years

First King of the Ten-Tribe King of Israel. The son of Nebat, one of Solomon's officers in the village of Zeredah of the tribe of Ephraim. Apparently at an early age Jeroboam was left fatherless, to be raised by his widowed mother Zeruah. (I Kings 11:26).

When Solomon observed that Jeroboam was not only a valiant mighty man but also a hard worker, he was put in charge of the compulsory labor force of the house of Joseph. (I Kings 11:28) subsequently God's prophet Ahijah approached him with startling news. After tearing his new garment into twelve pieces the prophet told Jeroboam to take ten of them in symbol of how God would divide Solomon's Kingdom in two and make Jeroboam King over ten of the tribes.

This however, was to be merely a governmental division and not also a departure from true worship as centered at the temple in Jerusalem, the capital of the Southern Kingdom. So God assured Jeroboam that he would bless and prosper his reign and build him a lasting house of successors provided he kept God's law and commandments (I Kings 11:29-38).

Upon learning of these events by Solomon, Solomon sought to kill Jeroboam. Jeroboam fled to Egypt, and there under the shelter of Pharoah Shishak he remained until the death of Solomon (I Kings 11:40).

The news of Solomon death in 997 BC brought Jeroboam quickly to his homeland, where he joined his people in demanding that Solomon's son Rehoboam lighten their burdens if he wanted their support of his new kingship. Rehoboam, however, disregarded the good advise of the older counselors in preference to that of the younger companions who told him to increase the workload of the people. The Ten-Tribe responded to this harshness by making Jeroboam their king. In reality this "turn of affairs" took place at the instance God, in order that the might indeed carry out His word that God has spoken by means of the prophet Ahijah (I Kings 12:1-20, II Chronicle 10:1-19).

King Jeroboam immediately set about to build up Shechem as his royal capitol, and East of Shechem on the other side of the Jordan he fortified the settlement of Penuel (I Kings 12:25). Jeroboam decided to put a stop to his people giving allegiance to Jerusalem, so he establish a religion centered around two calves, one at Bethel in the South, the other at Dan in the North.
Jeroboam also set up his own non-Aaronic Priesthood, composed of those among the people in general who were willing to procure the office by offering one bull and seven rams. These men also served "for the high places" and for the goat-shaped demons and for calves that he had made. He also invented special "holidays" (I Kings 12:26-33); II Kings 23:15; II Chronicle 11:13-17; 13:9).

In the eighteenth year of Jeroboam's reign Rehoboam died, but the warring that had gone on between the two nations continued during the three year reign of Rehoboam's son Abijam who succeeded him (I Kings 15:1,2,6; II Chronicle 12:15). Jeroboam had many calamities in his life (I Kings 14-15 Chapters). In 976 BC. God dealt a blow to Jeroboam and he died, bringing an end to his twenty-two year reign (II Chronicle 13:20). His son Nadab succeeded him to the throne for two years before being killed by Baasha, who also cut off every breathing thing of Jeroboam's house, according to "God word" and an account of the sins of Jeroboam. (I Kings 15:25-30).

As the Northern Kingdom continued on their spiritual decline, the Prophet Hosea and Amos had some harsh criticism to offer Jeroboam and his supporters for their outright apostasy. (Hosea 1:2, 4:1-2, 12-17; 5:1-7; 6:10) (Amos 2:6-8; 3:9, 12-15; 4:1).

# King Nadad

Reign 2 Years

Son of Jeroboam and second King of the Northern ten-tribe Kingdom of Israel. Nadab ruled parts of two years (976-975 BC) during which he continued the calf worship instituted by his father. While beseiging Gibbethon, a former Levite city (Joshua 21:20, 23) taken over by the Philistines, Nadab was assassinated by Baasha, who then killed off all remaining members of Jeroboam's house in order to secure the throne for himself. (I Kings 14:20; 15:25-31).

*From the days of Nadab King of Israel, Gibbethon a Levitic City, a sore spot on the border of Philistine Ekron later King Omri stabilized the kingdom and strengthened it against Aram. (I Kings 16:16).*

# King Baasha

Reign 24 Years

Third King of the ten-tribe Kingdom of Israel, Son of Ahijah of the tribe of Issachar and of insignificant background. He usurped the throne by killing his predecessor Nadab, after which he struck down the entire house of Jeroboam, as had been prophesied. (I Kings 15:27-30; 14:10). Baasha, however, continued Jeroboam calf worship, and for this his own house also was promised extermination. (I Kings 16:1-4). When he waged war against Judah, Asa induced the King of Syria to harass Baasha from the North, the fortified city of Ramah, which Baasha was building Asa then razed (I Kings 15:16-22, II Chronicle 16:1-6). After having ruled twenty-four years (975-952 BC), Baasha died and was buried in his capital Tirzah. His son Elah succeeded him, but in two years Zimri rebelled and wiped out Baasha house, fulfilling God's decree (I Kings 16:6-13).

*King Baasha fortified Ramah, on the main central highway, some five miles from Jerusalem. War among the Aramean Kingdom became Israel most serious rival. These blows forced Baasha to retreat from Judah and return to Tirzah, which had become the capital of Israel, perhaps at the end of the reign of Rehoboam (I Kings 14:17)*

*"And they carried away the stones of Ramah and its timber, with which Baasha had been building; and with them King Asa built Geba of Benjamin and Mizpah."*

# King Elah

Reign 2 Years

Fourth King of the Northern ten-tribe Kingdom of Israel. Elah came to the throne on the death of his father Baasha and ruled in Tirzah for parts two years, about 952-951 BC (I Kings 16:8) while Elah was drunk, Zimri, the Chief over half the chariots, put him to death to get the kingship for himself and then went on to wipe out all of Baasha house, to fulfil God's prophecy (I Kings 16:1-14).

Chapter 16

Execution done at last, Baasha's son Elah, like Jeroboam's son Nadab, reigned two years and then was slain by Zimri, one of his own soldiers Verse 3, Verse 9, 10 death comes easily upon men when they are drunk.

# King Zimri

Reign 7 days

Fifth King of the ten-tribe Kingdom of Israel. Zimri ruled Tirzah for seven days in about 951 BC. He had previously been Chief of half chariot under Elah, but when the army was away at Gibbethon, and King Elah had remained behind, Zimri killed him and all the rest of his household, and made himself king. His rule was very short because the army made Omri king and immediately returned to beseige Tirzah, where upon Zimri burned the king house down over himself. Zimri is noted for doing what was bad in God's eyes (I Kings 16:3, 4, 9-20).

Chapter 16:15-28
*Zimri and Tibni and Omri are here striving for the crown. Proud aspiring men ruin one another, and involve others in the ruin Verses 17-18. Then Omri and all the Israelites with him withdrew from Gibbethon and laid siege to Tirzah-When Zimri saw that the city was taken, he went into the Citadel of the Royal Palace and set the place on fire around him. So he died.*

# King Tibni

Reign 3 Years

A contender for kingship of the ten-tribe Kingdom of Israel, following the seven-day rule of Israel fifth King Zimri in 951 BC. The populace was divided over whether Tibni or Omri should now be king. Three years later, during which time civil war presumably raged, the issue was finally settled. Tibni lost to Omri supporters and met death. He was the son of Ginath (I Kings 16:15, 21-23).

# King Omri

Reign 11 Years

The sixth king of the northern ten-tribe Kingdom of Israel. Nothing of Omri's ancestry is recorded, not even the name of his father or tribe. Omri founded the third dynasty of Israel (those of Jeroboam and Baasha preceded), his son Ahab and grandson Ahaziah and Jehoram succeeding him, all four totaling some forty-six years (951-905 BC) on the throne. Omri's granddaughter Athaliah ruled six years on the throne of Judah (II Kings 8:26; 11:1-3; II Chronicle 22:2).

Omri came to the throne, not by inheritance, but by the sword. He had been chief of Israel's army under King Elah (and perhaps under his predecessor Baasha) when Zimri, chief of half the chariots, overthrew King Elah, took the kingship for himself and wiped out the house and friends of Baasha. As soon as this was reported to the Israelite army, at the time thy camped against the Philistines at Gibbethon, "all Israel doubtless the tribal heads in the camp," made Omri their king. They withdrew from Gibbethon and stormed Zimri's capital Tirzah. Zimri, seeing the hopelessness of his cause, burned down the king's house over himself, tragically ending his seven-day rule (I Kings 16:8-20). But a new rival to Omri presented himself-Tibni the son of Ginath. The populace remained divided for four years, during which time civil war presumably raged until Omri's supporters defeated Tibni. Tibni died in some unstated way, leaving Omri eight years of sole rule, down to the thirty-eight year of Asa (940 BC) (I Kings 16:21-23, 29) Omri wisely moved his capital away from Tirzah, which he found so easy to capture. He purchased the mountain owned by Shemer, well suited for fortifying, and built there a new city, Samaria, which was able to withstand long sieges (I Kings 16:23, 24). In the course of his reign Omri met with various setbacks, such as having to surrender some cities to the King of Syria. (I Kings 20:34) he was buried in Samaria (I Kings 16:28).

# King Ahab

Reign 22 Years

Son of Omri and a king of the Northern Kingdom of Israel. He ruled in Samaria twenty-two years, from 940 to 919 BC, and was succeeded at his death by his son Ahaziah (I Kings 16:28, 29; 22:40, 51).

Ahab's record was one of the worst as regards to the vital area of true worship. Not only did the corrupted worship of God by means of Jeroboam's golden calves continue, but Ahab also allowed Baal worship to infect Israel on an unprecedented scale due to his early marriage to Jezebel, the daughter of Ethbaal, King of Sidon. Ahab allowed his pagan wife Jezebel to lead him into Baal worship, to build a temple for Baal and a sacred pole in honor of Ashtoreh. Before long there were four hundred and fifty Prophets of Baal and four hundred Prophets of the Sacred Pole, all being fed from Jezebel royal table (I Kings 16-18:19). True prophets of God were slain by the sword and only the action of Ahab's house manager Obadiah, a man of faith, preserved the life of one hundred of them by hiding them in caves, where they lived on bread and water. (I Kings 18:3,4, 13, 19:10). As a result of his turning to Baal worship, Ahab was informed by Elijah of the coming of a severe drought which covered a period of three years and six months (I Kings 17:1; 18:1). Only at Elijah word the rains would return, and though Ahab searched for him in all the surrounding nations and kingdom, Elijah stayed out of reach until the due time (I Kings 17:8, 9; 18:2, 10).

Ahab had now endeavored to place the blame on Elijah for the drought and famine, an accusation that Elijah refuted, showing the real cause to be the Baal worship patronized by Ahab test held on top of Mount Carmel proved Baal to be nonentity and manifested God as being the true God; the prophet Baal was slain at Elijah's command, and shortly thereafter a drenching down pour brought on end to the drought (I Kings 18:17-46). Ahab headed back to Jezreel and to his wife, whom he informed of Elijah's actions against Baalism. Jezebel reacted with a violet threat to Elijah, resulting in his flight to Mount Horeb (I Kings 19:1-8).

During a three year interval of peace, Ahab turned his attention to the acquisition of the vineyard of Naboth of Jezreel, a piece of land much desired by Ahab because it bordered his residential palace grounds there. When Naboth refused the request on the basis of God's law regarding the inviolability of hereditary possessions, Ahab was angry and withdrew to his couch with his face to the wall, refusing to eat. Learning the cause of his dejection, Pagan Jezebel arranged the murder of Naboth under guise of a trial for blasphemy, using letters written in Ahab's name. When Ahab went to take possession of the vineyard he was met by Elijah. Elijah denounced him as a murderer and as one who sold himself to wickedness at the constant prodding of his pagan wife. As the dogs licked up Naboth's blood so dogs would lick up Ahab blood and Jezebel herself and Ahab's descendant would become food for dogs and scavenger bird. These words hit home, and in deep grief Ahab fasted in sackcloth, alternately sitting and pacing the floor. Ahab's relation with Judah to the South strengthen through a marriage alliance in which Ahab's daughter was married to King Jehoshaphat's son Jehoram (I Kings 22:44;II Kings 8:18, 26), II Chronicle 18:1). During a visit by Jehoshaphat to Samaria, Ahab induced him to support him in a effort to retake Ramothgilead from Syria. With this negotiation, false prophet gave the assurance of success, but one prophet Micaiah hated by Ahab predicted certain calamity. Ordering Micaiah's arrest, Ahab stubbornly went ahead with the attack, though taking the precaution to disguise himself, but he was hit by a Syrian archer so that he slowly died. His body was brought back to Samaria for burial and when they began to wash off the war chariot by the blood of Samaria.... The dogs went licking up his blood.

# King Ahaziah

Reign 2 Years

Son of Ahab and Jezebel and King of Israel for two years (920-918 BC.). He followed his idolatrous parent in Baal worship (I Kings 22:51-53). Upon the death of his father, Moab seized the opportunity to revolt and thereby free itself from the heavy tribute of one hundred thousand lambs and an equal number of male sheep with their wool (II Kings 1:1; 3:4, 5).

Ahaziah did form a maritime alliance with Jehosphaphat of Judah for a ship building enterprise at Ezion-geber on the gulf of Agabah. The project was disapproved by God due to Ahaziah's wickedness, and the ships became wrecked. (II Chronicle 20:35-37). The account of I Kings 22:48, 49 shows that Ahaziah wanted Jehoshaphat's authorization for Israelite mariners to man the ship jointly along with those of Judah, a request that Jehosphaphat refused, it may have been that Jehosphaphat acknowledged that God disapproval of the project.

A house incident, in which King Ahaziah fell through a grating (perhaps on covering a daylight shaft) in his roof chamber, left him bedridden and seriously ill. (II Kings 1:2)

As if the true God no longer existed, Ahaziah sent messengers to inquire of the Philistines god Baal-Zebub (Lord or owners of flies) as to his prospects of recovery. Intercepted by the prophet Elijah, the messenger turned back and delivered the message to the king that his sickbed would become his deathbed. Instead of humbling himself, Ahaziah sent a force of fifty men under their captain to bring Elijah to him. That force and a second one were both destroyed by the fire upon approaching the mountain where Elijah was. A third force barely escaped only by virtue of the captain's respectful plea that he and his men live. Elijah thereafter descended and delivered the death message to Ahaziah face. Ahaziah gradually died and being sonless was succeeded by his brother Jehoram.

# King Jehoram

Reign 12 Years

Son of Ahab and Jezebel, who succeeded his older brother Ahaziah as the tenth king of the Northern Kingdom of Israel in about 917 BC. He reigned twelve years, until about 905 BC (II Kings 1:17, 18, 3:1; 9:22). This King of Israel should not be confused with the King of Judah by the same name; who was his brother-in-law. Though Jehoram removed the sacred pillar of Baal erected by his father, he continued to do "what was bad in God's eyes," clinging to calf worship instituted by Jeroboam (I Kings 12:26-29; 16:33).

King Jehoshaphat of Judah and the king of Edom joined Jehoram in an attack on Moab that proved successful because God deceived the enemy with an optical illusion. God's prophet Elisha instructed those of the camp of Israel to dig ditches in which to catch much needed and divinely provided water. The next morning the reflection of the sunlight upon the water caused the Moabites to think the water was blood. The Moabites thinking that camp of Israel, Edom and Judah to be killed, they moved in to take the spoil, only to be slaughtered in great numbers (II Kings 3:4-27).

Naaman, the army chief of Syria, came to Jehoram to be cured of leprosy, bearing a letter to that effect from the King of Syria. Jehoram in reply, said "Am I God who can put to death and preserve alive and cure leprosy?"

Elisha, however, requested that Jehoram send Naaman to him, so that the Syrian army chief might know that the true God did have a prophet in the land, one capable of performing such cures (II Kings 5:18) despite such manifestation of God's loving kindness, Jehoram, down to the day of his death did not repent and turn to God with all his heart.

Death came suddenly and in an unexpected way. While recuperating from wounds received in a battle with the Syrian, he went out to meet Jehu, asking "Is there peace, Jehu? The negative answer made Jehoram turn to flee, but Jehu shot an arrow through his heart thus "this son of a murderer" (II Kings 6:32) was executed, his dead body being pitched into the field of Naboth (II Kings 9:14-26).

# King Jehu

Reign 28 years

The son of Jehoshaphat (not Jehoshaphat of Judah) and grandson of Nimshi. (II Kings 9:14) Jehu ruled as King of Israel for about 905 to 876 BC. During the reign of King Ahab of Israel, Elijah the prophet fled to Mount Horeb to escape death at the hands of Ahab's wife Jezebel. God commanded Elijah to go back and anoint three men: Elisha as Elijah successor, Hazael as King of Syria and Jehu as King of Israel. (I Kings 19:15, 16). God timed the anointing exactly right, when the opportunity was ripe for Jehu to put the anointing immediately in effort by action. The due time came. It was a time of war. Ahab was now dead and his son Jehoram was ruling. Israel's army was gathered at Ramoth-gilead, keeping guard against forces of Hazael King of Syria. Jehu was there as one of the military commanders (II King 8:28; 9:14). As the Israel's military force kept guard at Ramoth-gilead, Jehoram of Israel was recovering from wounds he had received from the Syrians. Elisha called one of the sons of the prophets, his attendant, telling him to take a flask of oil, to go to the Israelite camp at Ramoth-gilead, there anoint Jehu and flee. Elisha's attendant obeyed, calling Jehu away from the other officers into a house, where he anointed him and stated Jehu's commission to destroy the entire house of Ahab. (II Kings 9:1-10). The men saw Jehu appearance and knew something significance had occurred. On being pressed Jehu revealed that he had been annointed as King of Israel.

The destruction of the house of Ahab for Jehu wasted no time in pursuing the completion of his mission (II King 9:17-28) (II Chronicle 22:6-9). On Jehu arrival in Jezreel, Ahab's widow Jezebel called out: "Did it go all right with Zimri, the killer of the Lord?" But Jehu unmoved by this veiled threat, called upon the official to throw her down. She fell and her blood spattered on the wall and Jehu trampled her under his horses. Likely to keep the ten-tribe Kingdom of Israel distinct from the Kingdom of Judah with its temple of God at Jerusalem, King Jehu let the calf worship remained in Israel with its centers at Dan and Bethel, and Jehu himself did not take care to walk in the law of God of Israel with all his heart. He did not turn aside from the sins of Jeroboam with which he caused Israel to sin. God had promised Jehu that four generations of his sons would sit upon the throne of Israel. This was fulfilled in Jehu's descendants Jehoahaz, Jehoash, Jeroboam II and Zechariah, whose rule ended in his assassination in 791 BC. The dynasty of Jehu therefore reigned over Israel for about 114 years. (II King 10:30; 13:1, 10; 14:23; 15:8-12).

The real power of the Kingdom of Israel was broken when Jehu's house fell, the kingdom lasting only about fifty years longer, only Menahem, who struck down Zechariah's murderer Shallum, had a son succeeding him on the throne. This son Pekahiah was assasinated, as was his murderer and successor Pekah. Hoshea, Israel's last King, went into captivity to the King of Assyria. II King 15:10, 13-30; 17:4).

# King Jehoahaz

Reign 17 Years

King of Israel, son and successor of King Jehu for seventeen years. Jehoahaz reigned from 876 to about 860 BC (II Kings 10:35; 13:1). When he succeeded his father to the throne, much of the realm was controlled by Syria King Hazael of Damacus, who had seized from Jehu all of Israel's territory East of the Jordan River (II Kings 10:32-34) and because Jehoahaz did what was bad in God's eyes, God allowed Hazael to continue to oppress Israel all the days of Jehoahaz, reducing his fighting force to a mere fifty horsemen, the chariots and ten thousand foot soldiers.

Finally, Jehoahaz sought God's favor and because of the covenant with Abraham, Isaac and Jacob, God did not allow Syria to bring Israel completely to ruin (II Kings 13:2-7, 22, 23). Upon his death Jehoahaz was buried in Samaria and was succeeded on the throne by his son Jehoash (II Kings 13:8; 9, II Chronicle 25:17).

# King Jehoash

Reign 16 Years

King of Israel, son of Jehoahaz and grandson of Jehu. He ruled for sixteen years in the middle of the ninth century BC. During the first part of the reign of Jehoash the (son of Jehoahaz) over the northern Kingdom  Joash (sometimes written Jehoash) the son of Ahaziah was king over the Southern Kingdom of Judah (II Kings 13:10). Jehoash did what was bad in God's eyes and allowed calf worship to continue throughout the land nevertheless, when the prophet Elisha was sick and near death, Jehoash wept over him saying, " O my father, my father, the war chariot of Israel and his horsemen." (II Kings 13:11, 14). In response to the prophet's request Jehoash shot an arrow out the window toward Syria, and then beat the earth with his arrows. However he only beat three times. Elisha was incensed at this for had he continued to beat the earth five or six times. Elisha said, then Jehoash would have been completely victorious over the Syrians, but now the prophet declared, he would enjoy only three partial victories (II Kings 13:15-19) Jehoash captures three Israelites cities from Syrian (II Kings 13:24, 25). With a war between Israel and Judah (II Kings 14:8-14) (II Chronicle 25:17-24) Jehoash died and was buried in Samaria and his son Jeroboam II ruled in his place.

# King Jeroboam II

Reign 41 Years

King of Israel, son and successor of Jehoash, and great-grandson of Jehu. As the fourteenth ruler of the Northern Kingdom Jeroboam II reigned for forty-one years from about 843to 802 BC (II Kings 14:16, 23). Like so many of his predecessors he did what was bad in God's eyes by perpetuating the calf worship of Jeroboam I (III Kings 14:24) However, the outstanding achievement of his reign was the restoration of land that had earlier been lost by the kingdom. In fulfillment of Jonah's prophecy Jeroboam, "restored the boundary of Israel from the entering in of Hamath clear to the Sea of Arabah (Dead Sea)". He is also credited with restoring "Damascus and Hamath to Judah in Israel" (II Kings 14:25-28). This may mean that Jeroboam made the Kindom of Damascus and Hamath tributary, as they had once been to Judah during the reigns of David and Solomon. (Compare II Samuel 8:5-10; I Kings 4:21; II Chronicle 8:4).

In the wave of his successes came harsh criticism from the prophets Hosea and Amos because of the Northern Kingdom spiritual decline. Jeroboam and his supporter continued their outright apostasy, as well as immoral conduct, fraud, thievery, fornication, murder, oppression, idolatry and other God-dishonoring practices (Hosea 1:2, 4; 4:1, 2, 12-17; 5:1-7, 6:10) (Amos 2:6-8; 3:9, 12-15; 4:1).

Amos warned Jeroboam II that by the mouth of God, he would die by the sword (Amos 7:9-11). After his death, his son Zechariah ascended the throne (II Kings 14:29). However, there was a gap of eleven years between Jeroboam and the six months rule of Zechariah, the last of Jehu dynasty.

# King Zechariah

Reign 6 Months

King of Israel, Zechariah was a son of Jeroboam II and the last of Jehu dynasty to rule.  His recorded reign of six months was terminated when he was murder by Shallum.  (II Kings 15:8-12) Zechariah father died in 803 BC, in the 27th year of Uzziah reign (II Kings 14:29), but some eleven years passed before his stated rule of six months duration occurred in Uzziah 38th and 39th years (792/791 BC).  (II Kings 15:8, 13).  This may have been due to considerable opposition (typical of the Northern Kingdom of Israel) that had to be overcome before he was firmly established in the kingdom.

# King Shallum

Reign 1 Month

Sixteenth King of the ten-tribe Kingdom; son of Jabesh. In a conspiracy Shallum killed Zechariah, the last of Jehu ruling descendants, and became king in Samaria for one lunar month-791 BC only to be murdered by Menahem (II King 15:8, 10-15).

# King Menahem

Reign 10 Years

Son of Gadi and King of Israel for ten years (791-780 BC). Upon learning that Shallum had assassinated King Zechariah, Menahem went from Tirzah to Samaria and killed the assassin there. He then assumed rulership. Evidently during the early part of his reign Menahem struck down Tiphsah, because it not open up to him. The town was apparently reluctant to open it gates to him-Harsh treatment was meted out to the populace. All pregnant women he ripped up (II King 15:10, 13-17). Menahem did what was bad in God's eyes. He promoted calf worship, failing to depart from the sin of Jeroboam. During his reign, King Pul (Tiglath- Pileser III) invaded Israel and Menahem was forced to pay that Assyrian monarch "a thousand talents of silver" equal to about $1,423,000. He gave the silver that was obtained from 60,000 persons and was thinking this will strengthen his hand but instead the King of Assyria withdrew. Menahem died about 780 BC and his son Pekahiah succeeded him on Israel's throne (II Kings 15:22).

# King Pekahiah

Reign 2 Years

King of Israel in Samaria, son and successor of Menahem.  His brief reign of two years (780-778 BC) was marked by the same idolatrous calf worship introduced by Jeroboam and permitted by Menahem.  Pekah conspired against Pekahiah, killed him and began to reign in his place (II Kings 15:22-26).

# King Pekah

Reign 20Years

King of Israel for twenty- years period (778-758-BC). He reign the same time the Judean Kings, Uzziah, Jotham and Ahaz. During Pekah's reign idolatrous calf worship continued. (II Kings 15:28) Pekah formed an alliance with Rezin, the King of Syria and both Pekah and Rezin caused trouble with Judah (II Kings 15:32, 37, 38) they did not succeed in dethroning the monarch by Judah and sustained heavy losses (II Kings 16: 1. 5), (Isaiah 7:1-7) many captives from Judah was returned back to Judah (II Chronicle 28:6, 8-15) Hoshea the son of Elah killed Pekah and became Israel's next king.

*II Chronicle 28:6, 10, 11*
*Verse 6 For Pekah the son of Remaliah killed one hundred and twenty thousand in Judah in one day, all valiant men, because they had forsaken the Lord God of their fathers.*

*Verse 10"And now you propose to force the children of Judah and Jerusalem to be your male and female slaves; but are you not guilty before the Lord your God?*

*Verse 11 "Now hear me, therefore, and return the captives, whom you have taken captive from your brethen, for the fierce wrath of the Lord is upon you."*

# King Hoshea

Reign 10 Years

Last King of the Northern Kingdom of Israel, which came to its end in 740 BC, son of Elah. He did what was bad in God's sight, yet not to the same degree as his predecessors (II Kings 17:1, 2) Hoshea had no hereditary claim to the throne, nor did he receive special anointing from God to be King rather, it was by conspiracy against and murder of King Pekah that usurper Hoshea put King Pekah to death.

It appears that Hoshea was not fully recognized as King over Israel until sometime later, however for the record of Assyrian King Tiglath, Pileser III make claim that he put Hoshea on the throne. Shalmaneser successor to Tiglath-Pileser, compelled Hoshea to pay tribute, but it was not long before Hoshea sent messengers to "So" the King of Egypt appealing for assistance and subsequently withheld tribute from the Assyrians. Upon learning the secret conspiracy, Shalmaneser put Hoshea in the house of detention and laid seige to Samaria in 742 BC. Nearly three years later, in 740 BC, the city fell its inhabitants were carried off into exile and the split-off Ten-Tribe Kingdom of Israel came to its end (II King 17:3-6).

# DIVIDED KINGDOM

KINGS OF JUDAH- Southern Kingdom (Two Tribes)

1. Rehoboam

2. Abijam

3. Asa

4. Jehoshaphat

5. Jehoram

6. Ahaziah

7. *Athaliah

8. Joash

9. Amaziah

10. Uzziah

11. Jothan

12. Ahaz

13. **Hezekiah

* Queen Athaliah, an usurper on the throne.
* *Hezekiah began his reign at the fall of the Northern Kingdom and the beginning of the Single Kingdom.

# King Rehoboam

Reign 17 Years

Son of Solomon by his Ammonite wife Naamah, he succeeded his father to the throne in 997 BC at the age of forty-one and reigned for seventeen years (I King 14:21; I Chronicle 3:10; II Chronicle 9:31) Rehoboam had the distinction of being the last king of the United Kingdom and the first ruler of the Southern two-tribes Kingdom of Judah and Benjamin. Rehoboam was crowned king at Shechem by all Israel, but what was once the United Kingdom at David and Solomon was now divided. The ten-tribe withdrew their support of Rehoboam and made Jeroboam their king, even as God by the prophet Ahijah had foretold (I King 11:29-31; 12:1; II Chronicle 10:1). This separation took place after a delegation of the people with Jeroboam as their spokeman, pleaded with Rehoboam to remove some of the oppressive measure laid upon them by Solomon. Rehoboam took the matter under advisement. First he consulted the older men who counseled him to heed the cry of the pople and reduce their burdens, thereby proving himself a wise king, loved by the people. But Rehoboam spurned this mature advice and sought the counsel of young men with whom he had grown up. They told the king he should in effect make his little finger as thick as his father's hips increasing their yoke burden and chastising them with scourges instead of whips. This arrogant high-handed attitudes adopted by Rehoboam completely alienated from him the majority of the people. The only tribes continuing to support the house of David were Judah and Benjamin, while the priests and Levites of both kingdoms, as well as isolated individuals of the ten-tribe also gave support (I King 12:16, 17; I Chronicle 11:13, 14, 16; II Chronicle 10:16,17).

For a time Rehoboam walked quite closely to the laws of God, and early in his reign he built and fortified a number of cities some of which he stocked with food supplies (II Chronicle 11:5-12, 17). However, when his kingship was firmly established he abandoned God's worship and led Judah in the practice of detestable sex worship, perhaps due to the Ammonite influence on his mother's side of the family. (I Kings 14:22-24, II Chronicle 12:1). This behavior provoked God's anger and in expression thereof He raised up the king of Egypt, Shishak who together with his allies, overan the land and captured a number of cities in Judah in the fifth year of Rehoboam's reign. Had it not been that Rehoboam and his princes humbled themselves in repentance, not even Jerusalem would have escaped. As it was, the treasures of the temple and the King's house, including the gold shields that Solomon had made were taken by Shishak as his booty. Rehoboam then replaced these shields with copper ones (I Kings 14:25-28; II Chronicle 12:2-12).

During his lifetime Rehoboam married eighteen wives, the favorite being Maacah, the granddaughter of David's son Absalom and the mother of Abijah (Abijam), one of his twenty-eight sons and heir apparent to the throne (II Chronicle 11:18-22).

Before his death at the age of fifty-eight, and the ascension of Abijam to the throne in 980 BC. Rehoboam distributed many gifts among his sons, presumably to prevent any revolt against Abijam after his death (I Kings 14:31; II Chronicle 11:23. 12:16). Rehoboam's life is best summed up as: "He did what was bad, for he had not firmly established his heart to search for God." (II Chronicle 12:14).

# King Abijam

Reign 3 Years

One of Rehoboam's twenty-eight sons, also called Abijah, who became the second King of the two-tribe Kingdom of Judah and reigned from 980 to 977 BC. (I Kings 14:31-15:8). He was a legal descendant of David on both his father's and mother's side, the sixteenth generation from Abraham in the royal lineage of Jesus Christ. (I Chronicle 3:10; Matthew 1:7). Of all Rehoboam's eighteen wives and sixty concubines, Maacah (called Micaiah in II Chronicle 13:2), the granddaughter of Absalom was his most beloved and favored above the others. Abijah not being the first son was chosen as successor to the throne because of the love for his mother (II Chronicle 11:20-22).

With the ascension of Abijah to the throne in the eighteenth year of King Jeroboam I of Israel, the hostilities between the Northern and Southern Kingdoms resumed and a bloody war ensued. Abijah condemned Jeroboam crowd for their idolatrous calf worship and reminding them that God's covenant with David was for a never-ending kingdom. "With us there is at the head the true God," declared Abijah, therefore "do not fight against God----for you will not prove successful," (II Chronicle 12:16; 13:1-12). Later Ahijah began to walk in the sins of his father Rehoboam by allowing the high places, sacred pillars and even the male temple prostitutes to continue in the land. His heart did not prove to be complete with God, (I Kings 14:22-24; 15:3). During his lifetime he had fourteen wives and thirty-eight children, and upon his death his son Asa succeeded him upon the throne (II Chronicle 13:21; 14:1).

# King Asa

Reign 41 Years

The third king of Judah following the division of the nation into two kingdoms. Asa was the son of Abijam and grandson of Rehoboam. Since his father's three year rule began in the eighteenth year (980 BC.) of the reign of Jeroboam I, King of Israel, and Asa's began in the twentieth year of Jeroboam. Abijam died before completing his third full year and Asa completed that year as an accession period, followed by his forty-one year rule (977-936 BC.) (I Kings 15:1, 2, 9, 10).

Asa's zeal for pure worship came twenty years since the nation split. His zeal for pure worship, "like David his forefather," he courageously set about to clean the male temple prostitutes and the idols of the land. He removed his grandmother, Maacah from her position as a sort of "first lady" of the land because of her making a "horrible idol" to the sacred pole of Asherah (I Kings 15:11-13). Asa removed all the high places worship, but it cropped up again and were not removed at the time of the conclusion of his reign, allowing for it to be smashed by his successor Jehoshaphat. Asa's zeal for right worship brought blessings of peace from God during his first ten years of reign (II Chronicle 14:1, 6). Total victory resulted when they went to war (II Chronicle 14:8-15). Asa is thereafter met by the Prophet Azariah who reminds him that " God is with you as long as you prove to be with Him," and "if you leave Him he will leave you." Asa's ready response and strengthening of the nations in true service to God results in a great number of persons from the Northern Kingdom abandoning that region to join in a grand assembly at Jerusalem in Asa's fifteenth year of rule (963 BC) at which assembly a covenant is made declaring their determination to seek God and providing the death penalty for those not keeping this covenant: (II Chronicle 15:8-15).

King Baasha of Israel tried to block others from returning to Judah, Asa by some process of human reasoning tried to stop this movement and failed to rely solely on God. For this, Asa was confronted by Hanani the seer who pointed out Asa's inconsistency in not leaning upon God who had delivered him from the vast Ethiopian force. For his foolishness, Asa would now face continued warfare. Resenting correction, Asa unjustly jailed Hanani and showed himself oppressive to others of the people (II Chronicle 16:7-11). Warefare continued between Asa and King Baasha all their days as Hanani had foretold (II Chronicle 16:9). Asa's last three years brought suffering due to an illness of the feet (perhaps gout), and he unwisely sought physical healing over spiritual healing. At his death he was given an honorable burial in his personally prepared tomb in the city of David. The forthy-one year reign of Asa touched or covered the reigns of eight Kings of Israel: Jeroboam, Nadab, Baasha, Elah, Zimri, Omri and Tibni. Upon Asa's death his son Jehoshaphats became King (I Kings 15:24).

# King Jehoshaphat

Reign 25 Years

Son of Judean King Asa by Azubah the daughter of Shilhi. At the age of thirty-five Jehoshaphat succeeded his father to the throne and ruled for twenty-five years. (936-911 BC) (I Kings 22:42; II Chronicle 20:31). His good reign was contemporaneous with that of Israelite Kings Ahab, Ahaziah and Jehoram (I Kings 22:41, 51; II Kings 3:1, 2; II Chronicle 17:3,4). It was marked by stability, prosperity, glory and relative peace with neighboring lands. Jehoshaphat received presents from his subjects and tribute from the Philistines and Arabs (II Chronicle 17:5, 10, 11).

Jehoshaphat manifested great concern for true worship (II Chronicle 17:4). He commissioned certain princes, Levites and priest to teach God's Law in the cities of Judah (II Chronicle 17:7-9). Jehoshaphat also sanctified holy offering and personally traveled throughout his realm, directing his subjects to return to God in faithfulness. (II Chronicle 19:4) Jehoshaphat continued to compaign against idolatry and high places, but inproper worship was so entrenched among the Israelites that Jehoshaphat's effort did not completely and permanently eradicate it. (I Kings 22:43; II Chronicle 20:33).

Jehoshaphat's reign also witnessed the institution of a better judicial system, he impressed upon the judges the importance of being impartial and free from bribery, since they were judging, not for man, but for God. Jehoshaphat proved himself to be a king who relied fully on God. When the nation was threatened by the enemies, God fought for Judah and then the surrounding nations became fearful and Judah continued to enjoy peace (II Chronicle 20:1-30). Jehoshaphat maintained peace with the Northern Kingdom and formed a marriage alliance with Ahab (I Kings 22:44; II Chronicle 18:1).

Jehoshaphat barely escaped with his life when he went to battle because of the agreement he made with King Ahab (I Kings 22:2-37, II Chronicle Chapter 18). Upon returning to Jerusalem,

Jehoshaphat was censured for unwisely allying himself with wicked King Ahab (II Chronicle 19:2).

While Jehoshaphat was still alive he gave the kingship to his first born Jehoram, but to his other sons he gave precious gifts and fortified cities in Judah. (II Kings 8:16; II Chronicle 21:3) After Jehoshaphat death and burial the marriage alliance he made with Ahab prove to be disastrous to the house of Judah. Queen Athaliah (not appointed as queen) had influence in the house of Judah. (I Kings 22:50; II Chronicle 21:1-7, 11).

# King Jehoram

Reign 8 Years

The firstborn son of Jehoshaphat who, at the age of thirty-two, became king of Judah. (II Chronicle 21: 1-3, 5, 20). It appears that for some five years prior to this Jehoram may have been co-ruler of Judah with his father. (II Kings 1:17; 8:16) as sole ruler of Judah he reigned eight years from 913 to 905 BC (II Kings 8:17).

During these times of Jehoram's reign both the Northern and Southern Kingdoms had rulers with the same name. They were also brothers-in-law due to the fact that Jehoram of Judah married Athaliah, the daughter of Ahab and Jezebel and sister of Jehoram of Israel (II Kings 8:18, 25, 26). At least partially due to the bad influence of his wife Athaliah, Jehoram did not pursue the righteous ways of his father Jehoshaphat (II Kings 8:18) Jehoram not only murdered his six brothers and some of the princes of Judah, but also turned his subjects away from the true God to false gods (II Chronicle 21:1-6, 11-14). His whole reign was marred by both internal trouble and external strife. First Edom rebelled; then Libnah revolted against Judah (II Kings 8:20-22). In a letter to Jehoram, the prophet Elijah warned: "Look! God is dealing a great blow to your people and to your sons and to your wives and to all your goods." Moreover, you King Jehoram, "will be with many sickness, with a malady of your intestines," (II Chronicle 21:12-18). It all occurred just that way. God allowed Arabs and Philistines to overrun the land and take Jehoram's wives and sons captive. God permitted only Jehoram's youngest son Jehoahaz (also called Ahaziah) to escape, only for the kingdom covenant made with David. After all this God plaqued Jehoram in his intestines with a sickness for which there was no healing. Two years later the intestines came out and he gradually died. He was buried in the city of David, but not in the burial places of the kings. Ahaziah his son became king in his stead (II Chronicle 21:7, 16-20; 22:1; II Chronicle 3:10, 11).

# King Ahaziah

Reign 1 Year

Son of Jehoram and Athaliah and listed as a King of Judah for one year (905 BC). During his father's reign the Philistines and Arabs invaded Judah and took captive all Jehoram's son except Ahaziah, the youngest. (II Chronicle 21:16, 17; 22:1)

Jehoram was a young man of twenty-two years when ascendng to the throne and his domineering mother Athaliah, daughter of King Ahab and Jezebel, influenced him to wickness (II King 8:25-27; II Chronicle 22:2-4). He accompained King Jehoram of Israel (his maternal uncle) in a fight against Syria at Ramoth-Gilead, which resulted in Jehoram's being wounded. Later Ahaziah visited the convalscence Jehoram at Jezreel. (II King 8:28, 29; 9:15; II Chronicle 22:5,6) Jehu, on nearing Jezreel met Jehoram and Ahaziah. Jehu struck down Jehoram but Ahaziah fled at this time. Jehu did not pursue Ahaziah, but continued to Jezreel to finish his execution there. Meanwhile after the fleeing Ahaziah tried to make his way back to Jerusalem; however, he only got as far as Samaria, where he tried to hide. Jehu men pursuing Ahaziah, discovered him in Samaria and captured him. They brought him to Jehu, who was near the town of Ibleam, not far from Jezreel. Jehu ordered his men to kill him in his chariot. They struck him but Ahaziah was allowed to escape, and fled to Megiddo, where he died of his wounds. He was then taken to Jerusalem and buried there.

# Queen Athaliah

Reign 7 Years

Queen of Judah, daughter of King Ahab of Israel and his wife Jezebel, and granddaughter of Omri (II Kings 8:18, 26). She is the sister of Israel King Jehoram, and sister or half sister of the other seventy sons of Ahabs, all of whom Jehu ordered killed (II Kings 3:1, 2; 10:1-9). Athaliah was given in a marriage of political expediency to Jehoram, the eldest son of Jehoshaphat of Judah (II Kings 8:27; II Chronicle 18:1). She was the mother of Ahaziah, who was the King of Judah before her reign.

Like her mother Jezebel, Athaliah egged on her husband Jehoram to do what was evil in God's eyes during his eight-year reign (I Kings 21:25; II Chronicle 21:4-6). And like her mother, Athaliah want only to shed the blood of the innocent. When her wicked son Ahaziah died after a one-year reign, she killed off all the others of the royal line, except the infant Jehoash, who had been hidden by the high priest and his wife, who was Jehoash's aunt. Athaliah then installed herself as Queen for six years (904-898 BC) (II Chronicle 22:1). During this time she robbed God's temple of the holy things and offered them up to Baal.

When Jehoash reached seven years of age, God fearing High Preist Jehoiada brought the lad out of secrecy and crowned him rightful heir to the throne. Hearing the Tumult, Athaliah rushed to the temple and, upon seeing what was happening, cried, "conspiracy!" High Priest Jehoiada order her taken outside the temple grounds to be executed at the horsegate of the palace; she was perhaps the last of Ahab's Abominable house (II Kings 11:1-20; II Chronicle 22:1-23:21).

# King Joash

Reign 40 Years

Joash sometime written as Jehoash, King of Judah for forty years from 898 to 858 BC. He was the youngest son of Judah's King Ahaziah. His mother was Zibiah from Beersheba. (II Kings 12:1; I Chronicle 3:11). The death of Ahaziah gave Athaliah, the wicked grandmother of Joash, an excuse to make herself Queen. To prevent anyone in the future from challenging her seizure of the throne. She killed off all the sons of Ahaziah with the exception of young Joash, who at that time was an infant less than a year old. He escaped the massacre because his Aunt Jehosheba, the wife of the high preist Jehoiada, took him and his nurse and secretly hid him in the temple for six years. When the child reached seven years of age. They took into his confidence five chieftains to who he revealed for the first time the legal heir to the throne. Jehoiada then armed the five hundred men under the command of the chieftains with shield and weapon from the temple and instructed them stand guard around Joash coronation in the temple courtyard. Anyone, attempting to interfere was to be killed (II Kings 11:4-12, 21; II Chronicle 23:1-11). Upon hearing the people shouting, Athaliah came running, at the same time crying, "Conspiracy! "Conspiracy!" She was quickly ushered out at the entry of the horsegate and they put her to death. Jehoiada then made a covenant of faithfulness between God, the newly installed King and the people. After which they tore down the house of Baal and destroyed its altar and images and even killed Mattan the Priest of Baal (II Kings 11:13-20; II Chronicle 23:12-21).

Thereafter, as long as High Priest Jehoiada lived and acted as father and adviser to Joash, the young Monarch prospered. Joash married by the time he was twenty-one, he had two wives, one of them whom was name Jehoaddan who had sons and daughters. In this way the line of David, leading to Messiah, which had come so near to being completely severed, was once made strong again. (II Kings 12:1-3; II Chronicle 24:1-3; 25:1). Joash saw the need to repair the temple, due to the neglect and plunder during the reign of

Athaliah, he urged the Levites to raise money for restoration (II Kings 12:9-16; II Chronicle 24:8-14).

After the death of faithful High Priest Jehoiada being 130 years, the princes of the realm gradually turned King Joash and the people away from God to the worship of pagan idols. God raised up prophets to warn them but they refused to give heed (II Chronicle 24:20-22). Retribution was not long in coming. With God's protection removed, a small military force at Syrians lead by Hazael was able to invade Judah's territory forcing Joash to give over the gold and treasures of the sanctuary, as well as his possession leaving him a broken and diseased man (II Kings 12:17, 18). Two of Joash servant formed a conspiracy and put Joash to death at the age of forty-seven. They buried him in the city of David with his forefathers (II Kings 12:19-21-21; II Chronicle 24:25-27).

# King Amaziah

Reign 29 Years

King of Judah who, in 858 BC. came to the throne at twenty-five and ruled for twenty-nine years from the assassination of his father Joash until his own death in 829 BC. His mother was Jehoaddin, his wife Jecoliah (II Kings 14:1, 2; 15:2; II Chronicle 25:1; 26:3). With the kingdom firmly in hand, he executed those that murdered his father, but he heeded the law of Moses not to punish their sons. His reign was marked by some enthusiam for true worship, but not with a "complete heart," and not without serious shortcomings that brought disaster both to himself and the nation of Judah. The record of his rule deals primarily with two military campaigns (II Chronicle 25:2), His first success was against the Edomites, using a force of 300,000 from Judah and Benjamin. God also gave Amaziah a smashing victory in the Valley of Salt, allowing him to kill off 20,000 of the enemy, and capture Sela (Petra) which he rename Joktheel. However, Amaziah brought the gods of Edom and began worshipping them, causing God's anger to blaze against him: "Why have you searched for the people's gods that did not deliver their own people out of your hand?" Amaziah only compounded the injury by silencing God's prophet. (II Kings 14:7; II Chronicle 25:16) Amaziah second compaign was tragic from start to finish. Towns from Judah were raided. Amaziah refuses to listen to God's prophet; apparently being puffed up with his recent victory God has doomed Amaziah to defeat due to his idolatry. The battle was joined at Beth-Shemesh; Judah fled; Amaziah was captured; a breach of about 583 feet was made in Jerusalem wall and a great amount of temple treasures and hostages were carried back to Samaria (II Kings 14:8-14; II Chronicle 25:13, 17-24). From the time that Amaziah turned away from God's worship a conspiracy was formed against him that finally forced Amaziah to flee Lachish. There the conspirators put him to death. Amaziah was succeeded by his sixteen-year old son Uzziah (Azariah) (II Kings 14:17-21; II Chronicle 25:25-28).

# King Uzziah

Reign 52 Years

King of Judah, also called Azariah. The son of Amaziah by his wife Jecoliah, Uzziah is credited with a reign of fifty-two years (829-777 BC). During this period Jeroboam II, Zechariah, Shallum, Menahem, Pekahiah and Pekah ruled in Succession over the Northern Kingdom. (II Kings 15:1, 2, 8, 10, 13, 14, 17, 23, 25, 27; II Chronicle 26:3). The Prophets Isaiah (1:1; 6:1), (Hosea 1:1) and (Amos 1:1) were contemporaries of Uzziah. This Kings'' reign witnessed an unusally great earthquake-Zech 14:5.

After the death of his father, sixteen-year old Uzziah was made King by the people of Judah (II Kings 14:21; II Chronicle 26:1). Uzziah became King on the twenty-seventh year of King Jeroboam II. It may be that in the twenty-seventh year of King Jeroboam the two-tribe Judean Kingdom was freed from subjection that perhaps began when Israelite King Jehoash defeated Uzziah's father Amaziah. (II Chronicle 25:22-24). So it maybe that Uzziah became a King a second time in a sense of being free from the domination of Israelite King Jeroboam II. Uzziah did what "was upright in God's eyes" this was largely due to this heeding the good instruction of a certain Zechariah (not the prophet) but his subjects continued improper sacrificing at high places. (II Kings 15:3; 4:2; II Chronicle 26:4,5). Uzziah became famous for military successes, attained with God's help. He restored Elath (Eloth) to the Kingdom of Judah and rebuilt that city located at the head of the Gulf of Agabah. He warred successfully against the Philistines, gained victories over the Arabian and Meurim. His powerful well-equipped fighting forces came to consist of 375,000 men under the control of 2,600 heads of paternal houses. He strengthened the fortifications of Jerusalem and built engines of war there (II Kings 14:22; II Chronicle 26:2-15). It appears that Uzziah's brilliant successes resulted in his becoming haughty to the point of invading the "Holy" compartment of the temple to burn incense. High Priest Azariah, accompanied by eighty underpriest, immediately followed the King into the temple and censured him for this unlawful act, urging him to leave the sanctuary. With the censer for burning incense in his hand and raging against the priests, Uzziah was miraculously stricken with leprosy in his forehead, whereupon the priests ushered him out of the temple. As an unclean leper Uzziah was cut off from all worship at the sanctuary and could not perform the kingly duties. He remained in a certain house until the day of his death, his son Jotham administered the affairs of state (II Chronicle 26:16-21). Uzziah was buried in the ground of a field connected with the royal cemetery rather that being placed in a rock-hewn tomb, maybe because of his leprosy.

# King Jotham

Reign 16 Years

Son of Judean King Uzziah by Jerusha, the daughter of Zadok (II Kings 15:32, 33; I Chronicle 3:12; II Chronicle 27:1; Matthew 1:9). Uzziah was struck with leprosy when he became angry with the priests because of being reproved by them for unlawfully invading the temple and attempting to offer incense. Jotham began caring for the kingly duties in his father's stead. After Uzziah's death Jotham at the age of twenty-five years being his sixteen year rule (777-762 BC) (IIKings 15:5, 7, 32; II Chronicle 26:18-21, 23; 27:8).

In the time of Jotham certain Gadites were enrolled genealogically, and Isaiah, Hosea and Micah served as prophets (I Chronicle 5:11, 17; Isaiah 1:1; Micah 1:1). Although his subjects engaged in improper worship at high places, Jotham personally did what was right in God's eyes (II Kings 15:35; II Chronicle 27:2, 6). Much construction work was done during Jotham's reign (II Chronicle 27:3-7). Jotham did not enjoy a peaceful reign, he warred with the Ammonites and finally triumphed over them and also experienced military pressures from Syria King Rezin and Israelite King Pekah (II King 15:37). At his death Jotham was buried in the city of David, and his son Ahaz, who had been about four years old when Jotham became king, ascended the throne of Judah (II Chronicle 27:7-28:1).

# King Ahaz

Reign 16 Years

The son of King Jotham of Judah. He began to reign at the age of twenty and continued for sixteen years until 745 BC. (II Kings 16:2; II Chronicle 28:1).

Isaiah, Hosea and Micah actively prophesied during Ahaz's reign but idolatry marked his reign. Ahaz not only allowed it among the people but also personally and regularly engaged in pagan sacrificing, to the extent of offering up his own sons in fire in the valley of Hinnom (II Kings 16:34; II Chronicle 28:34). Because of false worship Ahaz's rule was beset by a flood of troubles. Judah was invaded, many were slaughtered and some two hundred thousand Judean being taken captive. Only the intervention of the prophet Obed, with the support of certain leading men of Ephraim, cause these captives to be released to return to Judah (II Chronicle 28:5-15; 17-19; II King 16:5, 6; Isaiah 7:1) (II Kings 16:17, 18; II Chronicle 28:23-25). After sixteen years of misrule and rank apostasy, Ahaz died and though buried as his forefathers were "in the city of David" (II Kings 16:20) his body was not placed in the royal burial places of the Kings (II Chronicle 28:27).

# Single Kingdom
### (Southern- Two-Tribes)

## South

1. Hezekiah

2. Manasseh

3. Amos

4. Josiah

5. Jehoahaz

6. Jehoiakim

7. Jehoiachin

8. *Zedekiah

*The last King of Judah and the fall of Jerusalem (586 BC)

# King Hezekiah

Reign 29 Years

King of Judah, (745-716 BC). He apparently became king when his father Ahaz died, in the "third year of Hoshea "King of Israel (perhaps meaning Hoshea's third year as tributary King under Tiglath-Pileser III). Counting his reign officially from nisan of the following year (745 BC) (II Kings 18:1). Prophets contemporary with Hezekiah's reign were Isaiah, Hosea, and Micah (Isaiah 1:1; Hosea 1:1; Micah 1:1). Hezekiah was outstanding as a king who stayed near to God and done what was right in God's eyes. From the beginning of his reign he proved himself zealous for the promotion of true worship, not only in Judah, but in all the territory of Israel, God proved to be with him (II Kings 18:3-7). When Hezekiah came to the throne, the kingdom of Judah was under God's disfavor, for his father, Ahaz had committed many detestable acts before God and had left the false worship of pagan gods run unrestrained in Judah. Therefore, God had permitted the land to suffer at the hand of its enemies, particularly the second world power, Assyria. Ahaz stripped the temple and the palace to provide bribe for the king of Assyria. Hezekiah early in his reign "proceeded to rebel against the King of Assyria. At Hezekiah accession to the throne of Judah, the northern ten-tribe Kingdom of Israel was in worse condition. For their gross sins God had allowed them to come into dire straits, becoming tributary to Assyria , then Assyria would swallow up Israel and carry her people into captivity- (II Kings 17:5-23) (Judah became a single kingdom). Hezekiah demonstrated his zeal for God's worship immediately on taking the throne at the age of twenty-five years. He immediately reopen and repaired the temple and calling together the priests and Levites. He said to them: It is close to my heart to conclude a covenant with God the God of Israel. Many things taken place in the temple: organization of the Levites in their services, celebration of special Festival observed, the arrangement for musical instruments and singing of praises. The temple was cleansed and the utensil restored Hezekiah set of example by crushing to pieces the copper serpent that Moses had made, because the people had made it an idol, by burning sacrificial smoke to it (II Kings 18:4).

In those strenuous times, when Assyria was sweeping everything in its path, Hezekiah trusted in God. Hezekiah rebelled against the King of Assyria and struck down the Philistines cities, which had evidently become allied with Assyria. (II Kings 18:7, 8). Hezekiah stood courageously against the King of Assyria, he was doubtless strengthened by the prophet Isaiah (Isaiah 31:1; II Kings 19:5-9).

It was in Hezekiah's third year that Shalmaneser of Assyria began the siege of Samaria. After holding out for three years Samaria was taken, perhaps by Sargon II, Shalmaneser successor in 740 BC. The people of the ten-tribe kingdom were deported, the Assyrians moving in others to occupy the land (II Kings 18:9-12). This left the kingdom of Judah, representing God's theocratic government and true worship, like a small island surrounded by hostile enemies.

Sennacherib, Sargon's son was ambitious to add the conquest of Jerusalem to his trophies of war. In the fourteenth year of Hezekiah reign (732 BC) Sennacherib came up against all the fortified cities of Judah and proceeded to seize them. Hezekiah offered to buy Sennacherib off to save the threatened city of Jerusalem. Hezekiah was obliged to give all the silver that was found in the temple and the royal treasury. He had it laid on the temple doors and posts. This satisified the King of Assyria, but only temporarily (II Kings 18:13-16).

In the face of imminent attack by greedy Sennacherib, Hezekiah displayed wisdom and military strategy. He stopped up all the springs and water sources outside the city of Jerusalem, so that, in event of a siege, the Assyrians would be short of water supplies. He strengthened the city's fortifications and also his military equipment. He also encouraged the people to be courageous and strong. "For with them is an arm of flesh, but with us there is God, to help us and fight our battles." (II Chronicle 32:1-8).

Assyria continued to threat and taunt Hezekiah and God. Hezekiah was greatly distressed, but continued to trust in God. A report from Isaiah (Isaiah 37:1-7) said Sennacherib would return to his land and be slain (II King 19:1-7). Around the time of Sennacherib's threat against Jerusalem, Hezekiah was struck down with a malignant boil. He was instructed by the prophet Isaiah to arrange his affairs in preparation for death. At this time Hezekiah had not yet had a son, and it therefore appeared that the royal Davidic line was in danger of being broken. Hezekiah prayed to God fervently, with tears, whereupon God sent Isaiah back to inform Hezekiah that he would have fifteen years added to his life. A miraculous sign was given, the shadow of the sun being cause to move ten steps backward. Hezekiah had a son, Manesseh who later succeeded him on the throne II Kings 20:1-11, 21; 21:1; Isaiah 38:1-8, 21).

Babylonia King Berodach-Baladan (Merodach-Baladan) who were sent to Hezekiah after he recovered from his illness, Hezekiah may have displayed all this wealth to impress the King of Babylon as a possible ally against the King of Assyria. This, of course tend to excite the greed of the Babylonians when Isaiah heard how Hezekiah treated the Babylonian messenger He utter the inspired prophecy from God that the Babylonian in time would carry away everything into Babylon, including some of Hezekiah descendants. Hezekiah, however humbled himself and God Kindly allowed that the calamity would not come in his days (II Kings 20:12-19; II Chronicle 32:26, 31: Isaiah 39:1-8).

# King Manasseh

Reign 55 Years

King of Judah who was the son and successor of King Hezekiah. (II Kings 20:21; II Chronicle 32:33). Manasseh's mother was Hephzibah. He was twelve years old when he ascended the throne as the fourteenth King of Judah after David and rule for fifty-five years (716-661 BC) in Jerusalem. (II Kings 21:1). He did what was bad in God's eyes, rebuilding the high places His father had destroyed, setting up altars to Baal, worshiping "all the army of the heavens," and building false religious altars in two temple courtyard. He made his sons pass through the fire, practiced magic, employed divination and promoted spiritistic practices. Manasseh also put the graven image of the sacred pole he had made into the house of God. He seduced Judah and Jerusalem to do worse than the nations that God had annihilated from before the Son of Israel (II Kings 21:2-9; II Chronicle 33:2-9). Though God sent prophets these were not heeded, Manasseh was also guilty of shedding innocent blood in great quantity (II Kings 21:10-16), which according to the literature of the Jewish rabbis, included that of Isaiah, who they say was sawed apart at Manasseh command-compare Hebrews 11:37.

Manasseh was punished for paying no attention to God's message, the King of Assyria taking him captive to Babylon, one of the Assyrian Monarch's royal cities (II Chronicle 33:10, 11). While in captivity, Manasseh repented, humbling himself and praying to God. God heard his request for favor and restored him to the kingship in Jerusalem. (II Chronicle 33:12, 13) Manasseh thereafter built an outer wall for the city of David, put military chiefs in Judah fortified cities and removed the foreign gods and idol image from God's house, as well as the altars he had built in the mountain of the house of God and in Jerusalem.

Manasseh prepared the altar of God and began to sacrifice upon it, encouraging others also to serve God. However, the people were still sacrificing on high places. (II Chronicle 33:14-17). At

Manasseh death, he was succeeded in the kingship by his son Amon
(II Chronicle 33:20).

# King Amon

Reign 2 Years

A King of Judah and son of wicked King Manasseh. He began to rule at the age of twenty-two years (661 BC) and followed the idolatrous course of his father's earlier years. The bad conditions described at Zephaniah 1:4; 3:4) doubtless were developing at this time. After two years on the throne he was murdered by his own servants (659 BC). The people put the conspirators to death, placed his son Josiah on the throne, and buried Amon in the garden of Uzza (II King 21:19-26; II Chronicle 33:20-25).

# King Josiah

Reign 31 Years

Son of Judean King Amon by Jedidah the daughter Adaiah (II Kings 22:1) Josiah had at least two wives, Hamutal and Zebidiah (II Kings 23:31, 34, 36). Of his four sons mentioned in the Bible, only the first born, Johanan, did not rule as King over Judah (I Chronicle 3:14, 15).

After the assassination of his father and the execution of the conspirators eight-year old Josiah became King of Judah. (II King 21:28, 24, 26; II Chronicle 33:25) some six years later Zebidah gave birth to Josiah's second son, Jehoiakim (II Kings 22:1; 23:26). In the eighth year of his reign, Josiah sought to learn and do God's will (II Chronicle 34:3). It was also about this time that Jehoahaz (Shallum), Josiah's son by Hamutal, was born (II Kings 22:1; 23:31; Jeremiah 22:11).

During his twelfth years as King, Josiah began a campaign against Idolatry that apparently extended into the eighteenth year of his reign. Altars used for false worship were torn down and desecrated by burning human bones upon them. Also, sacred poles, graven image and molten statues were destroyed. Josiah even extended his efforts as far as the northern part of what had been territory of the Ten-Tribes Kingdom but had been desolated because of the Assyrian conquest and subsequent exile (II Chronicle 34:3-8). Evidently Zephaniah's and Jeremiah's denunciations of idolatry had a good effect (Jeremiah 1:1, 2; 3:6-10; Zephaniah 1:1-6).

After King Josiah completed cleansing the land of Judah and while he was having God's temple repaired, High Priest Hilkiah found the book of God's law by the hand of Moses, doubtless the "original copy." Entrusted by Hilkiah with this sensational find, Shaphan the secretary reported on the progress of the temple work and thereafter read the book to Josiah. On hearing God's word this faithful King ripped his garment apart and then commissioned a five-man delegation to inquire of God in his behalf and in the behalf of the people. The delegation went to the prophetess Huldah, then dwelling in Jerusalem and brought back a report to this effect: "calamity will come as a consequence of disobedience to God's law. But because you King Josiah, humbled yourself, you will be gathered to your graveyard in peace and will not see the calamity (II Kings 22:3-20; II Chronicle 34:8-28). Subsequently, Josiah assembled all the people of Judah and Jerusalem, including the older men, the priest and the prophets, and read God's law to them. After this they concluded a covenant of faithfulness before God.

In fulfillment of a prophecy uttered about three hundred years previously by an unnamed man of God, Josiah pulled down the altars built by Israel King Jeroboam at Bethel, not only at Bethel but also in the other cities of Samaria. The high places and altars were removed (I Kings 13:1, 2; II Kings 23:4-20; II Chronicle 35:1-9). About four years later Josiah became father to Mattaniah (Zekediah) by his wife Hamutal-(II Kings 22:1; 23:31, 34, 36; 24: 8, 17-18). Toward the close of Josiah's thirty-one year reign (659-629) Pharoah Necho led his armies northward to fight the "King of Assyria", for a reason not revealed in the Bible, King Josiah disregarded a divine warning and tried to turn the Egyptian forces back at Megiddo but was mortally wounded in the attempt. He was brought back to Jerusalem in a war chariot and died enroute or upon arrival. All the people of Judah and Jerusalem mourned over Josiah (II Chronicle 35:20-25; II Kings 23:29, 30). Although three of Josiah's son and one grandson ruled as king over Judah, none of them imitated his fine example of turning to God (II Kings 23:25-37; 24:8, 9, 18, 19).

# King Jehoahaz

Reign 3 Months

King of Judah; fourth son and successor of Josiah. His mother name was Hamutal ( II Kings 23:31) Ezra and Jeremiah according to certain manuscripts, called him Shallum, which some suggest may have been his name prior to his accession to the throne. (I Chronicle 3:15; Jeremiah 22:11). After the death of his father at the hand of Pharoah Necho of Egypt, Jehoahaz, the youngest son of Josiah, was apparently the people's choice as successor to the throne (II Kings 23:29, 30). In II Chronicles 36:2, where this same event is mentioned, certain translation have his name shortened to Joahaz for Jehoahaz.

Jehoahaz was twenty-three years old when made king, and ruled badly for three months in the early part of the year 628 BC, until he was imprisoned at Riblah by Pharoah. Later he was taken to Egypt, where he died in captivity, just as the prophet Jeremiah had foretold (II Kings 23:31-34; Jeremiah 22:10-12).

# King Jehoiakim

Reign 11 Years

One of the last Judean Kings, son of Josiah by Zebidah, and originally called Eliakim (II Kings 23:34, 36; I Chronicle 3:15). Jehoiakim had rule of about eleven years (628-618 BC) was marked by injustices, oppression and murders (II Chronicle 36:5; Jeremiah 22:17; 52:2). Also during his reign Judah experienced harassment from Chaldeans, Syrian, Moabite and Ammonites (II Kings 24:2).

After the death of King Josiah, the people of Judah for some reason constituted Eliakim's younger brother Jehoahaz King. About three months later Pharaoh Necho took King Jehoahaz captive and made twenty-five year old Eliakim King, changing the new ruler name to Jehoiakim Pharoah Necho also imposed a heavy fine on the Kingdom of Judah. Jehoiakim in turn oppressed the people with heavy taxation. Jeremiah, pronounced woe upon this wicked ruler, indicating that he would have the burial of a he-ass (Jeremiah 22:13-19) (II Kings 23:34-36; II Chronicle 36:35). Early in Jehoiakim reign Jeremiah warned that unless the people repented Jerusalem and her temple would be destroyed. Thereafter the prophet was threatened by death. However, the prominent man Ahikam stood up for Jeremiah and saved the prophet from harm. Previously another Prophet, Urijah prophecy enraged Jehoiakim and he did not escape the kings' wrath (Jeremiah 26:1-24).

The fourth year of Jehoiakim reign (625 BC) Nebuchadnezzar defeated Pharaoh Necho in a battle over domination of Syria-Palestine. In that same year Jeremiah began dictating to his secretary Baruch God's word directed against Israel, Judah and all the nations, recording messages that had begun to be delivered from the thirteenth year of Josiah's reign (at which time Jehoiakim had been about six years old). The scroll containing the dictated message was read before King Jehoiakim. As soon as Jehudi read three or four page columns, that section was cut off and thrown into the fire burning in the brazier of the King's winterhouse. Thus the entire scroll was put in the flame section by section. Jehoiakim ignored the pleas of three of his princes not to burn the scroll. He particularly objected to the prophetic words that pointed to the desolation of Judah at the hands of Babylon's King. This suggests that Nebuchanezzar had not yet come against Jerusalem and made Jehoiakim his vassal (Jeremiah 36:1-4, 21-29).

Second Kings 24:1 shows that Nebuchadnezzar brought pressure upon the Judean King and so Jehoiakim became his servant (or vassal) for three years.

Following the siege of Jerusalem during Jehoiakim's third year (as Vassal King), Daniel and other Judeans, including nobles and members of the royal family were taken as exiles to Babylon. There being no record of an earlier Babylonian exile, this appears to place the event in the short reign of Jehoiachin, Jehoiakim successor. (II Kings 24:12-16, Jeremiah 52:28).

After Jehoiakim's son Jehoiachin surrender, Nebuchadnezzar elevated Jehoiachin's uncle Zedekiah to the throne of Judah. (II Chronicle 36:9, 10). This fulfilled Jeremiah's prophecy that Jehoiakim would have no one sitting on the throne of David (Jeremiah 36:30) Jehoiakim's son Jehoiachin ruled a mere three months and ten days (II Chronicle 36:9) God's prophecy through Jeremiah (22:18, 19; 36:30) indicated that Jehoiakim was not to receive a decent burial; his corpse was to lie unattended outside the gates of Jerusalem exposed to the suns heat by day and the frost by night.

# King Jehoiachin

Reign 3 Months

Son of Judean King Jehoiakim by Nehusta (II Kings 24:6, 8; II Chronicle 36:8). He is also called Jeconiah and Coniah (Jeremiah 28:4; 37:1).

At the age of eighteen Jehoiachin became King and continued the bad practices of his father. (II Kings 24:8, 9; II Chronicle 36:9) Jehoiachin's father Jehoiakim, had been under subjection to Babylonian King Nebuchadnezzar, but rebelled in his third year of such vassalage (618 BC) (II Kings 24:1). This resulted in a siege being laid against Jerusalem. It appears that Jehoiakim died during this siege and Jehoiachin ascended the throne of Judah. His rule ended, however, a mere three months and ten days later, when he surrendered to Nebuchadnezzar (617 BC) (II Kings 24:11, 12; II Chronicle 36.9). In fulfillment of God's word through Jeremiah, he was taken into Babylonian captivity. (Jeremiah 22:24-27; 24:1; 27-19, 20; 29:1, 2). Other members of the royal household, court officials, craftmen and warriors were also exiled (II Kings 24:14-16).

It appears that Nebuchadnezzar, after successfully conquering Jerusalem, returned to Babylon and from there sent and proceeded to bring Jehoiachin and desirable articles from Jerusalem.

Nebuchadnezzar retired to Riblah in the land of Hamath, leaving the post-conquest details to his chief of the bodyguard, Nebuzardan (II Kings 25:8-21).

While in Babylon, Jehoiachin fathered seven sons (I Chronicle 3:16-18). In this way the royal line leading to the Messiah was preserved. (Matthew 1:11, 12). But as prophecy had indicated, none of Jehoiachin's descendants ever ruled from earthly Jerusalem. (Jeremiah 22:28-30). In the fifth year of Jehoiachin's exile, Ezekiel began his prophetic work. (Ezekiel 1:2). About thirty-two years later in 580 BC., Jehoiachin was released from prison by Nebuchadnezzar successor Evilmerodach and given a position of favor above all the other captive Kings, he receive daily allowance (II Kings 25:27-30; Jeremiah 52:31-34).

# King Zedekiah

Reign 11 Years

Last of the Judean King and the son of Josiah by his wife Hamutal. Upon his being constituted Vassal King, his name was changed by Babylonian King Nebuchadnezzar from Mattaniah to Zedekiah. During the eleven years of his reign Zedekiah "continuing to do what was bad in God's eyes (II Kings 24:17-19; II Chronicle 36:10-12; Jeremiah 37:1; 52:1, 2).

Zedekiah was about nine years old or about three years older than his nephew Jehoiachin. At that time the people made Zedekiah's full brother, twenty-three year old Jehoahaz, King. Jehoahaz' rule lasted only three months as Pharoach Necho removed him as King, replacing him with Eliakim (renamed Jehoiakim); the twenty-five year old half brother of Jehoahaz and Zedekiah. Following the death of his father Jehoiakim, Jehoiachin began ruling as King. It appears that at this time the Babylonians armies under King Nebuchadnezzar were besieging Jerusalem. After having reigned three months and ten days, Jehoiachin surrendered to the King of Babylon (617 BC) (II Kings 23:29-24:12; II Chronicle 35:20; 36:10). Subsequently Nebuchanezzar placed Zedekiah on the throne at Jerusalem and had him take an oath in God's name. This oath obligated Zedekiah to be a loyal Vassal King (II Chronicle 36:10, 11; Ezekiel 17:12-14).

Evidently, early in Zedekiah's reign messengers arrived from Edom, Moab, Ammon, Tyre and Sidon, perhaps with the intention of getting Zedekiah to join them in a coalition against King Nebuchanezzar (Jeremiah 27:1-3). The scriptures do not reveal just what the messengers accomplished. Possibly their mission did not succeed, as Jeremiah urged Zekediah and his people to remain submissive to the King of Babylon and also presented yoke bars to the messengers to symbolize the fact that the nations from which they have come should likewise submit to Nebuchadnezzar (Jeremiah 27:2-22).

Zedekiah personally went to Babylon in the fourth year of his reign. Likely this was to present tribute and thereby to reassure Nebuchadnezzar of his continued loyalty as Vassal King. On that occasion Zedekiah was accompanied by his quartermaster Seraiah, whom the prophet Jeremiah had entrusted with a scroll setting forth God's judgment against Babylon. (Jeremiah 51:59-64).

About a year later Ezekiel began serving as a prophet among the Jewish exiles in Babylonia (Ezekiel 1:1-3; compare II Kings 24:12, 17). In the sixth month of Zedekiah's sixth year as King (612 BC) Ezekiel saw a vision that revealed the idolatrous practices, including the worship of the god of Tammuz and the sun, being carried on at Jerusalem (Ezekiel 8:1-17). Three years later Zedekiah rebelled against Nebuchadnezzar and sent to Egypt for military assistant (II Kings 24:20; II Chronicle 36:13: Jeremiah 52:3; Ezekiel 17:15). This brought the Babylonian Armies under Nebuchadnezzar against Jerusalem. The siege of the city began in the ninth year in the tenth month of Zedekiah reign (Ezekiel 24:1-6). Words came from the Priests from Jerusalem to Jeremiah inquiring words of God. Whether Nebuchadnezzar would withdraw, (Jeremiah 34:1-7). Zedekiah continued to dispatch priests to Jeremiah with the request that the prophet pray to God in behalf of the people, so that the foretold destruction of Jerusalem would not come. But God's answer as conveyed by Jeremiah, showed that the divine judgement remained unchanged. The Chaldeans would return and destroy Jerusalem (Jeremiah 37:3-10). Later, when Jeremiah decided to leave Jerusalem to go to Benjamin, he was siezed at the gate of Benjamin and falsely accused of falling away to the Chaldeans. Jeremiah denied the charge, they did not listen to him and brought the prophet to the princes. This lead to Jeremiah's being imprisoned in the house of Jehonathan. After a considerable period had passed and Jerusalem again being besieged by the Babylonians, Zedekiah sent for Jeremiah. In reply to the King's inquiry, Jeremiah told Zedekiah that he would be given into the hand of the King of Babylon (Jeremiah 37:11-21; Jeremiah 38:1-28). Finally, in the eleventh year of Zedekiah, in the fourth month, on the ninth day of the month, Jerusalem was broken through. By night Zedekiah and the men of war took to flight. Overtaken in the desert plain of Jericho, Zedekiah was taken to Nebuchadnezzar at Riblah. Zedekiah's sons were slaughtered before his eyes. As Zedekiah was only about thirty-two years of age at that time, the boys could not have been very old. After witnessing the death of his sons, Zedekiah was blinded, bound with copper fetters and taken to Babylon, where he died in the house of custody- (II Kings 25:2-7; Jeremiah 39:2-7; 44:30; Jeremiah 24:8-10).

# Empire of Babylon
|

## Nabopolasser
### (Founder of Dynasty)

### Nebuchadnezzar
### (Son of Nabopolasser)

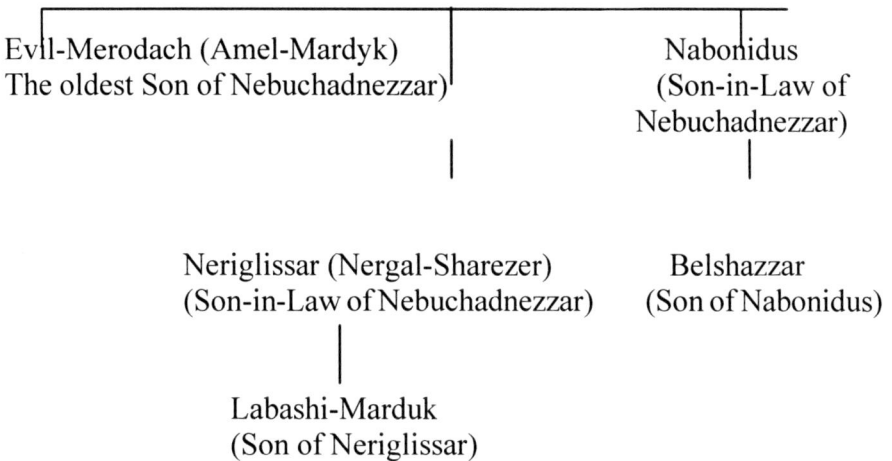

| | |
|---|---|
| Evil-Merodach (Amel-Mardyk) | Nabonidus |
| The oldest Son of Nebuchadnezzar) | (Son-in-Law of |
| | Nebuchadnezzar) |

| | |
|---|---|
| Neriglissar (Nergal-Sharezer) | Belshazzar |
| (Son-in-Law of Nebuchadnezzar) | (Son of Nabonidus) |

### Labashi-Marduk
### (Son of Neriglissar)

Nebuchadnezzar-

Nebuchadnezzar the Son of Nabopolasser and father of Evil-Merodach (Amel-Marduk), ruled as king for forty-three years (624-581 BC), this dates also include the "seven times" during which he ate vegetation like a bull (Daniel 4:31-33).

Evil-Merodach (also called Amel-Marbuk)

The oldest son of Babylonian King Nebuchadnezzar. He immediately succeeded to the throne in 580 BC. Evil-Merodach received mention in the Bible for the kindness he extended, in the year of his reign to Jehoiachin, the King of Judah, releasing him from the house of detention (II Kings 25:27-30), (Jeremiah 52:31-34).

<u>Neriglissar</u> (Also called Nergal Sharezer)

The successor of Evil-Merodach (Amel-Marduk). No other history of this King Only mention or found on Babylonian bricks, legal contracts and inscriptions.

# Babylonians Rulers

Labashi-Marduk
   Assassinated early in his reign, and Nabonidus succeeded him.

Nabonidus
   Last supreme Monarch of Babylonian Empire and father of Belshazzar. He ruled seventeen years of the seventy year exiles captives.

Belshazzar
   The first born son of Nabonidus and he reigned the last year of the Babylonian Empire (Daniel 5:11, 18, 22).

# Empire of Assyria
## (Assyrian's Rulers)

Tiglath- Pileser – A powerful King of Assyria, an Usurper of the throne. This King appears in the Bible as "Pul" (II Kings 15:19; I Chronicle 5:26). He reign about eighteen years.

Shalmaneser- Five different Assyrian Monarch bear this name. Only two appear to have contact with Israel: Shalmaneser III and Shalmaneser V Shalmaneser III succeed his father Ashurnasirpal known as the "Great Dragon" He made repeated thrusts to the West against the Aramean Kingdom in Syria.

Shalmaneser V-During the reign of Hosea (the last King of Israel) (748-740), Shalmaneser V advanced into Palestine and Hoshea became Vassal King under an imposition of annual tribute (II Kings 17:1-3). Hoshea failed to pay tribute and Samaria came under siege for three years and then the city fell and the Israelites were led into exile. Shalmaneser died or was murdered while the siege was in progress and Sargon II completed the conquest.

Sargon (Isaiah 20:1) The beginning reign of Sargon coincide with the fall of Samaria in the sixth year Judean King Hezekiah
.

Sennacherib (Son of Sargon and King of Assyria) Sennacherib's death is considered to have come some twenty years after his campaign against Jerusalem. Most of his years were served while Hezekiah was King (II Kings 18:17-35).

Esar-Haddon- A younger son and successor of Sennagherib King of Assyria (Isaiah 37:37, 38). He is also, mentioned in Ezra 4:2. The conquest of Egypt under Ethiopian ruler Tirhakah (II Kings 19:19). Upon Esar-Haddon's death Ashurbanipal became Assyria next Monarch.

Ashurbanipal (Asenappar)- The son of Esar-Haddon (Ezra 4-2) and grandson of King Sennacherib. His name also appears in Ezra 4:9-10.

# Egyptian Kings

## Shishak

An Egyptian known also as Sheshonk (I) from Egyptian records Shishak regarded as the founder of the "Libyan dynasty," and he ruled about twenty-one years. His son Osorkon (I) succeeded him. When Jeroboam fled to Egypt to escape the wrath of King Solomon, Shishak ruled I Kings 11:40). Some years later, in the fifty year of Solomon successor Rehoboam (992/993 BC) Shishak invaded Judah with a mighty force of chariots and horsemen. He captured fortified cities in Judah and then came to Jerusalem. But God did not allow him to bring Jerusalem to ruin, for Rehoboam and the princes of Judah humbled themselves upon receiving a message from the prophet Shemaiah. The city was not stripped (II Chronicle 12:1-12).

## "SO"

An Egyptian King contemporary with Hoshea, the last king of the Ten-Tribe Kingdom of Israel. When Hoshea conspired with "SO" against Shalmaneser and stopped paying tribute to Assyria. Hoshea was imprisoned (II Kings 17:3, 4).

## Tirhakah

During Hezekiah reign, while Assyrian King Sennachenrib was fighting against Libnah, news came that Tirhakah was on his way to fight the Assyrians (II Kings 19:8, 9; Isaiah 37:8, 9) Sennachenrib defeated the force that came from Egypt and captured "the Charioteers" of the King of Ethiopia". The next Assyrian King, Esar-Laddon boasted about his conquest of Egypt saying "Its King Tirhakah, I wounded five times with arrowshot and ruled over his entire country." Tirhakah was taken refuge and he was never heard of again.

## Necho(h)

A Pharoah of Egypt contemporaneous with the Judean King Josiah. Necho was the son of (Psammitichus, Psamtik I) and succeeded his father to the throne. Toward the close of Josiah's thirty-one year reign (659-629 BC) Pharoah Nechoh marched through Canaan to fight the "King of Assyrian" (the Babylonian conqueror of Assyria, Nabopolassar). At that time Josiah disregarded a divine warning and was mortally wounded while attempting to turn the Egyptian forces back at megiddo. About three months later Pharoah Nechoh took Jehoahaz, Josiah successor to the throne, captive and made twenty-five year old Eliakim his vassal, changing the new ruler's name to Jehoiakim. He impose a heavy fine on Judah (II Kings 23:29-35; II Chronicle 35:20, 36:4). Some four years later Nechoh's force suffered defeat at the hands of the Babylonians under the command of Nebuchadnezzar.

## Hoprha

Hophra was King of Egypt in the time of Zedekiah King of Judah and Nebuchadnezzar King of Babylon. It is believed to be Hophra with whom Zedekiah formed an alliance for protection against Nebuchadnezzar, contrary to the commands that God had given years before hand through Isaiah the prophet, warning Israel not to look to Egypt for help. (Isaiah 30:1-5; 31:1-3). Nebuchadnezzar came up against Jerusalem in 609 BC, but lifted the siege temporarily because of news that a military force was coming out of Egypt. The Egyptians disappointed Zedekiah, being forced to withdraw, and the Babylonians returned to destroy the city (Jeremiah 37:5-10). Jeremiah also foretold that Pharoah Hophra would be given into the hand of his enemies and into the hand of those seeking for his soul (Jeremiah 44:30). But his troops revolted and setup Amasis as rival King, later taking Hophra prisoner and finally strangling him to death.

# Syria Involvement during the
# Period of Kings of Israel and Judah

From and after the birth of Israel's monarchy, Syria became aggressively active militarily, and throughout the entire history of the Northern Kingdom hostilities between the two prevailed. King Saul went to war with the Syrian Kings of Zobah. (I Samuel 14:40 and David inflicted heavy losses on the army of Syrian King Hadadezer. David also set up garrisons in Damascus and compelled the Syrians to pay tribute. (II Samuel 8:3-12; I Chronicle 18:3-8).

After the death of Solomon and the dividing of his kingdom, it tells their reverse successes in their relations with the Israelites of both the Northern and Southern Kingdoms. For nearly three years there were no war between Syria and Israel ( I Kings 22:1).

God's prophet Elisha had certain contacts with the Syrians, as an example he cured the Syrian army Chief Naaman of leprosy (II Kings 5:1-20) and another occasion when a detachment of Syrians surrounded Dothan to take Elisha captive, the prophet first asked God to strike them with a form of blindness, and then led them to Samaria, where their vision was restored, had them fed and sent them home (II Kings 6:8-23). The Syrians were Semites, closely related and associated with the Israelites Aramaic was their language and the common Jew did not understand Aramaic (II Kings 18:26-28; Isaiah 36:11, 12).

# King Hazael

A notable King of Syria, Hazael apparently began to rule during the reign of King Jeroboam of Israel (917-905 BC) (II Kings 8:7-16). He died during the reign of King Jehoash of Israel (859-844 BC) (II Kings 13:24, 25) Hazael was not of royal lineage, but had been merely a high officer in the service of his predecessor, King Ben-hadad of Syria (II Kings 13:7-9).

Years prior to Hazael's reign, God had instructed Elijah to "anoint Hazael as king over Syria". The reason for the appointment was that Israel had sinned against God and Hazael was to execute punishment upon the nation. (I Kings 19:15-18).
Hazael was never literally anointed with oil, but the commission given to Elijah was nevertheless fulfilled by his successor Elisha the prophet. This occurred when Syrian King Ben-had , who had fallen sick, sent Hazael to Elisha, then in Syria's principal city, Damascus with a gift and an inquiry as to whether or not he would survive his sickness. Elisha said to Hazael: "Go say to Ben-hadad, you will positively recover, "but the prophet continued, saying: "And God has shown me that he will positively die: He further said to Hazael: "God has shown me you as king over Syria." ON Hazael's return, in reply to the King's question as to Elisha's answer, Hazael said: "He said to me, "you will positively revive," but then the next day, Hazael suffocated the king with a wet coverlet, and began to rule in his place (II Kings 8:7-15).

Shortly after becoming king, Hazael engaged in a war with the Kings of Israel and Judah at Ramoth-Gilead. At that time, King Jehoram of Israel was wounded at Ramah, but the outcome of the battle is not stated in the account (II King 8:25-29); (II Chronicle 22:1-6).
Hazael began to take Israel's land piece by piece, capturing Gilead and Bashan, East of Jordan. (II Kings 10:32, 33). This apparently opened the way for his later invasion of the Kingdom of Judah. Hazael took the city of Bath in Philistia, and then set his face to go up against Jerusalem. King Jehoash of Judah, however, bought Hazael off by giving him valuable things from the temple and

palace, so that Hazael withdrew, sparing Jerusalem. (II Kings 12:17, 18).

Hazael became a great oppressor of Israel, fufilling what the prophet Elisha had foreseen-that Hazael would consign Israel'' fortified places to the fire, kill their choice men with the sword, dash to pieces their children and rip up their pregnant women (II Kings 13:3, 22; 8:12). Yet God did not allow Syria to crush Israel completely. (II Kings 13:4, 5).

After Hazael's death, King Jehoash of Israel, in three victories, recaptured the cities that Hazael had taken away from King Jehoahaz, his father (II Kings 13:23-25).

# King Rezin

King of Syria who reigned in Damascus during parts of the reign of King Jotham (777-762 BC) of Judah and his son King Ahaz (whose reign ended about 746 BC). Evidently near the end of King Jotham's reign Rezin joined with Pekah the King of Israel in warring against Judah. (II Kings 15:36-38). During the warfare, which continued into the reign of Ahaz, the Sryians, evidently under Rezin captured many Judeans and took them to Damascus. (II Chronicle 28:5). Aslo, Rezin wrested from Judah Elath, a city on the Gulf of Agahah, clearing out the Jews and restoring the city to the Edomites (II Kings 16:16). The combined Syro-Israelite forces laid siege to Jerusalem, intending to make "the son of Tebeel" its king, but they were unable to capture the city (II Kings 16:5; Isaiah 7:1-6). The situation greatly frightened Ahaz, despite Isaiah's assurance that Rezin of Syria and Pekah of Israel need cause no fear. (Isaiah 7:3-12; 8:6, 7). Ahaz turned to Assyria for help, bribing Tiglath-Pileser III to attack Syria (II Kings 16:7, 8; II Chronicle 28:16, 20).

Tiglath-Pileser warred against Damascus, capturing it and putting Rezin to death. Syria thus came under Assyrian domination (II Kings 16:9).

# The Prophets and their Message

| Prophet | Date | Message to | | Rulers |
|---|---|---|---|---|
| Isaiah | 740 | Judah | Uzziah Jotham Ahaz | Jotham Ahaz |
| Jeremiah | 626 | Judah | Josiah, Zedekiah Johoiakim | Johoiakim |
| Ezekiel | 593 | Remnant in Judah and in Babylon | Nebuchadnezzar | Exile of Jehoiachin 5th Year |
| Daniel | 605 | Exile and Gentiles/Baby lon | Nebuchadnezza | Third year of Jehoiakim |
| Hosea | 750 | Israel | Jeroboam II, Jehoash,Hoshea | Uzziah, Jotham Ahaz/Hezekiah Judah |
| Joel | 830 | Judah | Joash | |
| Amos | 760 | Israel | Jeroboam II | Uzziah |
| Obadiah | 845 | Edom | Joram/Jehoram | |
| Jonah | 780 | Nineveh | Jeroboam II | |
| Micah | 735 | Judah | Jotham, Hezekiah | Ahaz |
| Nahum | 650 | Nineveh, Assyria | Manasseh | Josiah |
| Habakuk | 609 | Judah | Jehoiakim | |
| Zephaniah | 635 | Judah | Josiah | Manasseh |
| Haggai | 520 | Jews of the first return | Governor Zerubbabel | |
| Zechariah | 520 | Jews of the first return | Governor Zerubbabel | |
| Malachi | 430 | Jews in the Land of Israel | Governor Zerubbabel | |

# I Samuel

## Outline

I. Samuel The Prophet and Judge (Chapters 1-7)
- Samuel's Birth (Chapter 1)
- Hannah's Prayer Song, Eli's sinful sons (Chapter 2)
- The boy Samuel receives a call from God (Chapter 3)
- Eli's sons punished, Eli's death (Chapter 4)
- The Ark of the Covenant in Philistine hands, then returned to Israel, etc (Chapters 5-7)

II. Saul the king (Chapters 8)
- Israel's desire for a king (Chapter 8-15)
- Saul anointed king (Chapter 9-10)
- Saul defeat Ammon (Chapter 11)
- Samuel's retirement address: "…Serve the Lord with all your heart" (Chapter 12)
- Saul disobedience against God (Chapters 13 – 15).

III David enters the picture (Chapters 16-31)
- David anointed to be future king (Chapter 16)
- David and Goliath (Chapter 17)
- David and Jonathan (Chapter 18)
- David's life sought by Saul, etc. (Chapters 19-23)
- David spares Saul's life (chapter 24)
- Samuel's death, Nabal (Chapter 25)
- David spares Saul again, Saul confession (Chapter 26)
- David flees Saul (Chapter 27)
- Saul and the witch of Endor (Chapter 28)
- David's battles, Saul defeated and killed (Chapters 29-31)

# II Samuel

## <u>Outline</u>

I. David's reign at Hebron over Judah for seven and one-half years (Chapters 1-4)
- David's song of Lament over Saul and Jonathan (Chapter 1)
- David made king over Judah; Ishbosheth (Is-Bo-Sheth), Saul sons, King over
- Israel (Chapter 2)
- David is sought out by Abner, to become king over all Israel, but Abner is
- murdered (Chapter 3)
  Ishbosheth is killed (Chapter 4)

II. David's reign at Jerusalem over all Israel for thirty-three years (Chapters 5-24)
- David captures Jerusalem (Chapter 5)
- The Ark is brought to Jerusalem (Chapter 6)
- God's promise to David (Chapter 7)
- David extend the borders of his kingdom (Chapter 8)
- David is kind to Mephibosheth (Me-Fib-o-Sheth), Jonathan's son (Chapter 9)
- David defeats the Ammonites and the Syrians (Chapter 10)
- David sins against Uriah, Nathan's sharp words "you are the man" (Chapters 11-12)

- The Absalom events, Absalom's temporary defeat of David, Absalom's death,
- David mourns, "O my Son Absalom, my son, my son Absalom! (Chapters 13-18)
- David Mourns Absalom, Joab kills Amasa (Chapter 19)
- Sheba rebellion defeated (Chapter 20)
- Saul and Jonathan re-buried (Chapter 21)
- David's Song of Thanksgiving and deliverance (Chapter 22)
- David's Last Words, David Might Men (Chapter 23)
- David numbers Israel and Judah (Chapter 24)

# I King

## Outline

I. Solomon's Reign (Chapters 1-11)
- King David's last days (1:1-2:11)
- Solomon's reign begun (2:12)
- Solomon's Prayer for understanding (Chapter 3)
- Solomon's wise judgment and administration (Chapter 4)
- The building of the Temple (Chapter 5-7)
- (The Temple was arranged like the Tabernacle)
- The dedication of the Temple, Solomon's sermon and prayer (Chapter 8)
- God's promise to Solomon (Chapter 9)
- Solomon visited by the Queen of Sheba (Chapter 10)
- Solomon's sin, his punishment, and his death (Chapter 11)

II. Hostility and the divided kingdom: Rehoboam and Jeroboam to Ahad (Chapters 2-16:28)
- The ten tribes revolt, the kingdom divided North and South, Rehoboam reigns
- in the South, Jeroboam in the North (Chapter 12-14)
- Abijah and Asa reign over Judah (Chapters 15:1-24)
- Nadab reigns over Israel (Chapter 15:25-32)
- Baasha reigns over Israel (Chapter 15:33-16:7)
- Elah reigns over Israel (Chapter 16:8-14)
- Zimri reigns over Israel (Chapter 16:15-22)
- Omri reigns over Israel, Omri establishes capital at Samaria (Chapter 16:23-28)

III. The reign of Ahab, Elijah the Prophet (Chapter 16:29-22:53)
- Elijah fortells three year's drought but he is fed at brook Chenth: he raises the
- widow's son from the dead. (Chapters 16:29 –17:24)
- Contest: Elijah vs Prophets of Baal and the ensuing rain (Chapter 18)

- Elijah encouraged, "a still small voice" (Chapter 19)
- Ahab's victory over Ben-hadad, but Ahab's sin (Chapter 20)
- Ahab and Jezebel kill Naboth to get his vineyard (Chapter 21)
- Ahab killed in battle (Chapter 22)

# II Kings

## Outline

I.   Elisha The Prophet succeed Elijah (Chapters 1-12)
- Elijah's last days, his translation to heaven (Chapters 1-2)
- Elisha predicts victory over Moab (Chapter 3)
- Elisha performs miracles: Widow's Oil, son of the Shunamite raised from the
- dead, Naaman's leprosy cured, etc. (Chapters 4-5)
- Ben-hadad besieges Samaria (Chapter 6)
- Syria army flees (Chapter 7)
- Hazael becomes King of Syria (Chapter 8)
- Jehu made King of Israel, kills Jezebel and others (Chapter 9)
- Jehu executes the son of Ahab and wipes out the worship of Baal (Chapter 10)
- Athaliah captures Judah's throne for six years, then Joash become King (Chapter 11)
- Joash repairs the Temple (Chapter 12)

II. From the death of Elisha to the captivity of the Northern Kingdom (Chapters 13-17), Single Kingdom (Chapters 17-25)
- Elisha death (Chapter 13)
- The reign of Amaziah over Judah, Joash and Jeroboam II over Israel (Chapter 14)
- Uzziah (Azariah) reigns over Judah (52 years) followed by Jotham; Zachariah,
- Shallum, Menahem, Pekahiah, Pekah over Israel (Chapter 15)
- Ahaz reigns over Judah (Chapter 16)
- Assyria carries away Ten Northern tribes into captivity – (verse 18 from Chapter 17, "only the tribe of Judah was left."- The name "Jewish" appeared for the first time
- Single Kingdom began (Judah) (Chapter 17:18)
- Hezekiah, Manasseh, Amon, Josiah, Jehoahaz, Jehoiakim, and Jehoiachin reign. (Chapters 18-23)
- Zedekiah reign (Chapters 24-25)

# The Exile and Post-Exile Periods

The exile meant a complete readjustment, as deportation always does. The Jews were force to leave their homes give up deeds to property, and settle in a quiet foreign land. Once adapted to the new environment, however, the Jews proved their independence and creativity by entering the professions, involving themselves in international trade, and working in and with the banking systems. Upon the release of the Jews under Cyrus in 538, some were so well situated in business and their professions, and had their own homes-in a word, they were so well settled- that many did not leave for Jerusalem and their homeland. Many says that the Jews are still returning to their homeland and that is true as even today.

Cyrus, King of Persia, freed the Jews from Babylonish rule ('that the word of the Lord by mouth of Jeremiah might be fulfilled)" (II Chronicle 36:24-23; Ezra 1:1; Jeremiah 25:1-14) Jews went back on a volunteer basis, but with Persian guards.
Archaeological and textual evidence state that the southwest of Jerusalem. Southern Palestine came to be known as Idumea, for the Edomites had settled there after the Babylonian conquest.
The first great achievement of the returning exiles was the reconstruction of the temple, known as the Second Temple. The building had begun and was to be finished under Zerubbabel, Persian appointed governor of Jerusalem and Jew of the royal line, but subsequent interruptions delayed its completion. Finally, in 516 BC. And during the reign of Darius, it was finished.
The second great achievement was the reparation of the Walls of Jerusalem under Nehemiah. Men were organized into groups. Each group was responsible for completing the repairs of an assigned portion. The walls were completed, celebration of which event took place in 444 BC. The work had been strongly opposed by the Samaritans and the Ammonites.

CPSIA information can be obtained at www.ICGtesting.com
Printed in the USA
BVOW020019270912

301510BV00002B/9/A

9 780974 518879